TABLE OF CONTENTS

Unless otherwise indicated, all Scripture quotations are taken from the King James Version of the Bible.
Secrets of the Richest Man Who Ever Lived/B-99
ISBN-10: 1-56394-076-0
ISBN-13: 978-1563940767
Copyright © 2001 by **MIKE MURDOCK**
All publishing rights belong exclusively to Wisdom International
Publisher/Editor: Deborah Murdock Johnson
Published by The Wisdom Center · 4051 Denton Hwy. · Ft. Worth, Texas 76117
1-817-759-BOOK · 1-817-759-2665 · 1-817-759-0300
You Will Love Our Website..! WisdomOnline.com

Your Dream Is Closer Than It Has Ever Been In Your Lifetime.

-MIKE MURDOCK

WHY I WROTE THIS BOOK

Solomon was a master in achievements. Few men in history equal his magnificent works.

Thirty-one of those secrets are powerful and I wanted you to know them. Read and absorb the simple yet profound keys inside this book, *Secrets of the Richest Man Who Ever Lived.*

Your Dream Is Closer Than It Has Ever Been In Your Lifetime. The Golden Keys of Success are within your reach. In fact, they are inside this very book you are holding in your hand today.

If you have ever done something right, you are doing it now...holding this book in your hand.

Somebody *knows* something you do not know. Somebody has *done* something you have never done. Somebody *can help you* become everything you have ever dreamed of becoming...through the powerful Wisdom Keys and success secrets they have learned.

You do not need a lot of keys to enter a bank vault—just the *right* key. Little keys often unlock huge treasures.

Your life can *change.*

Your success can be *multiplied.*

That's why I wrote this book.

I really want you to succeed in life.

Make this your personal "Achiever's Handbook." Use your highlighter whenever necessary. Mark the book any way you desire to keep you reminded and focused on these golden principles of success. Use this book *continuously.*

Now go somewhere alone and lean back in your chair. *Relax.* Think and meditate about your Palace of Greatness—The Place you have always dreamed of being.

It is where you belong.

Mike Murdock

∽ 1 ∽

SOLOMON DECIDED TO DO SOMETHING THAT HAD NEVER BEEN DONE BEFORE

Solomon Was An Uncommon Achiever.
Uncommon Achievers are different.
In a doubting world, they *believe.*
In a slow world, they *run.*
In a weeping world, they *laugh.*
In a quitting world, they *persevere.*

Solomon is one of the most famous names in history. He wrote songs and collected proverbs. Kings begged for an appointment with him. He was brilliant, articulate and yet, very human.

He was the richest man who ever lived.

Solomon experienced tragic failures in his personal life, yet he rose to such prominence that even Jesus mentioned him thousands of years later in Matthew 6:29 and Matthew 12:42.

He was not a *perfect* man, but he was a *productive* man.

We are fascinated by his life. He experienced the magnetism of evil and fell into the web of immorality. He knew great gain and great loss.

He lived an incredibly full life.

He was wise. When God Himself permitted a temple to be built in His honor, He chose Solomon to oversee the work—and no one has produced its equal in the history of mankind.

How wealthy was Solomon?

Consider this.

In 1929, the Illinois Society of Architects did an extensive and meticulous study of the temple built by Solomon. Though the research was done almost seventy years ago, the experts placed its valued at $87 billion. When you figure in a 7 percent inflation rate per year, that places the value of the temple alone worth more than $500 billion. My friend Malcolm Burton has said that this amount is four times more than our nation spends on military defense each year. And that is just the beginning. It does *not* include Solomon's palace, his real estate holdings, and other valuable possessions too numerous to mention!

Think about it.

Today, the temple alone would be valued at more than $500 billion.

Now, think again.

What an *uncommon* achievement.

Have you ever stopped to consider the difference between $1 million and $1 billion? It has been said that a stack of $1,000 bills totaling $1 million would be 12 inches high. But, a stack of $1,000 bills totaling $1 *billion* would be taller than the Empire State Building!

That, my friend, is wealth.

Solomon's personal palace took almost twice as long to build, and is said to be equal in majesty and splendor. Is it possible even to imagine such wealth?

Solomon's life also included failure. What life has not? Scarred generals have a lot to teach naive soldiers. Any uncommon life is worth scrutiny.

Uncommon *leaders* are worth *knowing.*

Uncommon *kings* are worth *studying.*

Uncommon *dreamers* are worthy of pursuit.

Solomon was a dreamer. An effective dreamer. An unforgettable dreamer. An influential dreamer.

And, many dreamers are hurting inside these days.

Dreamers are often misunderstood.

Dreamers provide jobs and income for those who refuse to dream. They stretch the imagination of everyone around them. They thrust average people into the "zone of greatness." Yet they are often called money hungry, materialistic and greedy.

What really was the secret of the greatness of Solomon and his unequaled attainments? *His obsession for Wisdom.*

The answer is quite simple. Solomon's academic achievements have not been traced to an unusual genius. In fact, the opposite is true. In his dream, his inferiority rose like a monument. He knew how *limited* he really was within his own power. In 1 Kings 3:7, 9, we read the description of a man overwhelmed, "I am *but a little child:* I know not how to go out or come in. Give therefore Thy servant an understanding heart to judge Thy people, that I may discern between good and bad: for who is able to judge this thy so great a people?"

Solomon pursued Wisdom continuously. In Ecclesiastes 1:13, he says, "And I gave my heart to seek and search out by wisdom concerning all things that are done under Heaven."

Solomon mastered the "Principles of Achievement." He was much more than a dreamer. Yet he created a collection of monuments every uncommon dreamer should study and absorb. He *completed* his dreams and *no one has yet equalled his achievements*.

Your dream, too, is *obtainable*.

Your dream is *closer* than you can imagine.

Your dream, too, is necessary and essential.

Wake up. It is your turn to do something significant with your life, which is slipping between your fingers every hour and every minute of every day. I hope this dawns on you like the bursting of a million suns. I pray that it hits you hard.

When Solomon fueled the desire to build the temple, *God became involved.* Instructions were given, respected and followed.

No expense was spared.

It was meticulous and detailed.

Solomon decided to do something that had never been done before.

That is one of the Golden Secrets that helped him become The Richest Man Who Ever Lived.

☜ 2 ☞

SOLOMON DEVELOPED A PASSION FOR HIS DREAM

Solomon Knew What He Wanted.

Few people really know what they want. They do not realize that their dream is either *born* within them or *borrowed* from another. I have talked to many people who admit that their present pursuit is something their mother or father desired for them or was a convenient opportunity. Most people never pursue their own inner passion.

- ▶ Passionate people become *powerful* people.
- ▶ Passionate people generate *enthusiasm*.
- ▶ Passionate people create waves of *favor*.
- ▶ Passionate people stay *focused* on their dream.

Solomon had a passion to create a magnificent and incredible monument to God—the temple and house of the Lord. He did not consult a committee and he did not ask his nieces and nephews for confirmation. He did not present a survey to the neighboring leaders of other countries. Instead, he established a clear-cut goal, the building of the temple.

Do you really know what you want in life? What do you long to be remembered for when your life is over? What goal presently excites and *energizes* you? When you are alone and away from everyone else, what do you dream of becoming, doing or owning?

Passion is the best answer to pain. Learn to build your own Well of Blessing in the place where you are hurting the most. Uncommon achievers have learned to use the pain of their past to birth a passion for the future.

15 Facts That Will Help You Achieve An Uncommon Dream In Your Life

1. Dreams Are Born or Borrowed. Stop borrowing the dreams of others. Think creatively. Use your imagination. Think illogically for a few days. What would you *attempt* to do if you knew it was impossible to fail?

2. Your Dream May Require Encouragement From Others At First. But, eventually, your dream will so overwhelm you that you are motivating others to follow you!

3. Your Dream Does Not Always Require The Approval of Everyone You Love. Some will sneer, some will envy you, and others will be too self-absorbed to care.

4. Your Dream Can Start With Whatever Is In Your Heart Today. Big things always begin small. Acorns become oak trees.

5. You Already Have What It Takes To Launch An Uncommon Dream—DESIRE. Feed it and it will become a strong desire. Fuel it more and it will become an obsession. Your obsession will become the magnet that pulls others toward you to participate in your dream.

6. Your Dream Will Require A True Hunger For Obtainment. Have you ever watched a small child play with their food? He isn't really hungry. He prefers to get out of his high chair and run around the room with his little friends. Stop dabbling with your dream. You will never accomplish a dream without being "hungry."

7. Your Dream Must Become Your Magnificent Obsession. Many things are important, but an uncommon dream always determines what you do *first,* every day.

8. Your Dream Must Be Energizing Enough To Cause You To Make A Change In Your Daily Routine. Your dream must be unique enough to *attract* your attention, strong enough to *keep* your attention and deserving enough to qualify for your total focus.

9. An Uncommon Dream Will Require Immediate Attention. Move now. Move quickly and decisively. Avoid anything today that is temporary or faddish.

10. Your Dream Deserves Your Total Focus. Focus will keep you passionate, creative and persistent. It will remove the clutter of unnecessary appointments from your day. Passive people may find your presence uncomfortable. Your passion intimidates them. So, they look elsewhere to find someone to feed their lazy and sluggish walk through life.

11. Your Dream May Require A Geographical Change. Do you dream about being somewhere else? Where? Why aren't you moving toward it?

12. Your Dream Will Always Require The Assistance of Others. Who are the *top ten* people necessary to birth and complete this dream in your heart? Write down their names. What are your *expectations* of them? Be specific. Pinpoint exactly what you want them to do.

13. Your Dream May Require Extraordinary Negotiations With Others. Sam Walton did this. When he wanted to create the number one store in America, he went to his vendors. He negotiated with the owners of major companies for lower prices on their products.

He told them his plan and said, "I will need your cooperation." He insisted, fought and negotiated every inch of the way. He wanted to give his customers the best prices possible in America, and he required the same from the manufacturers of his products. He negotiated until he secured their cooperation, and they were rewarded with tremendous orders and profits.

Sam Walton knew the golden secrets necessary to make his own dream come true.

14. You Must Always Build Your Daily Agenda Around Your Dream. Schedule every appointment accordingly.

15. You Must Nurture And Protect Those Relationships Connected To Your Dream. Mention your dream in every telephone conversation. When friends request a gift list from you, give them a gift idea linked to the completion of your dream.

Dexter Yager is one of the most uncommon men I know. He is a true champion. I urge you to read his book, *Don't Let Anybody Steal Your Dream.* On page 33, Dexter writes, "The successful person associates with those who *support* his dream." Believe it!

Develop a passion for your dream like Solomon did. It is one of the Golden Secrets that helped him become The Richest Man Who Ever Lived.

≈ 3 ≈

Solomon Made Wisdom His Obsession

━━━▶━◯━◀━━━

Solomon Made Wisdom The Obsession And Goal of His Life.

Names are so important. They create mental pictures. When you hear someone speak the name of Thomas Edison, you think of inventions, don't you? Certainly. The name Henry Ford reminds you of automobiles. The Wright Brothers? Airplanes.

When Solomon's name is spoken, people think immediately of *Wisdom.* Why? *Wisdom was the obsession and goal of his life.* No other human on earth has ever been remembered for Wisdom comparable to his. Hundreds of years after his death, Jesus mentioned the Wisdom of Solomon. (See Matthew 12:42.)

Solomon's appetite for Wisdom was his significant *difference* from other men.

Thousands pursued wealth. Millions craved fame. Not Solomon. When he requested of God that Wisdom be his greatest gift, God responded with a remarkable statement in 1 Kings 3:11-13, "Because thou hast asked this thing, and hast not asked for thyself long life; neither hast asked riches for thyself, nor hast asked the life of thine enemies; but hast asked for thyself under-standing...lo, I have given thee a wise and an understanding heart; so that there was none like thee before thee, neither after thee shall any arise like unto thee. And I have also given thee that which thou hast not asked, both riches, and honour: so that there shall not be any among the kings like unto thee all thy days."

Solomon's success was not a hidden event; it was the talk of the earth.

World leaders begged for appointments with him. His counsel was treasured and followed. Moments in his presence became the golden memories of a lifetime for the greatest achievers of his day. The wealthy brought him unforgettable, unparalleled gifts.

Solomon sought the most important thing possible. Proverbs 4:7 says, "Wisdom is the principal thing." The ancient writings teach that the most important thing on earth is *Wisdom.* Solomon discovered that Wisdom produces *wealth,* gains *friendships,* and is more precious than gold and silver.

Solomon was aware of his greatness and even documented the *rewards* of his Wisdom.

Listen to this remarkable review of Solomon's accomplishments taken from Ecclesiastes 2:4-9, "I made me great works; I builded me houses; I planted me vineyards: I made me gardens and orchards, and I planted trees in them of all kind of fruits: I made me pools of water, to water therewith the wood that bringeth forth trees: I got me servants and maidens, and had servants born in my house; also I had great possessions of great and small cattle above all that were in Jerusalem before me: I gathered me also silver and gold, and the peculiar treasure of kings and of the provinces: I gat me men singers and women singers, and the delights of the sons of men, as musical instruments, and that of all sorts. So I was great, and increased more than all that were before me in Jerusalem: also my Wisdom remained with me."

Solomon knew failure, which often births Wisdom. He documented his deep depression and wrote about moments of indescribable pain. He was quite honest about it, never hiding his emptiness and moments of loss. "Therefore I hated life," he said in Ecclesiastes 2:17.

Solomon's father was King David, the illustrious warrior and psalmist. David wanted desperately to build the temple himself, but God personally selected Solomon. First Chronicles 17:11-12 says, "And it shall come to pass, when thy days be expired that thou must go to be with thy fathers, that I will raise up thy Seed after thee, which shall be of thy sons; and I will establish his kingdom. He shall build me an house, and I will stablish his throne for ever."

Solomon was the recipient of some of the most expensive gifts any human on earth ever received. One scholar said that when the Queen of Sheba wanted to hear his answers to her questions, she brought a gift of more than $4.5 million (120 talents of gold). First Kings 10 tells us that she came by chariot over 1200 miles through the mountains just to sit in his presence. Now, think about this for a moment. One of the wealthiest queens on earth brought a gift of $4.5 million in order *to secure an appointment with him.*

Why? Because Wisdom was Solomon's obsession. This Golden Secret helped him become The Richest Man Who Ever Lived.

The Atmosphere
You Permit
Determines The Product
You Produce.

-MIKE MURDOCK

❧ 4 ❧

SOLOMON CULTIVATED SELF-CONFIDENCE THAT HE COULD ACHIEVE HIS DREAM

Self-Confidence Creates A Climate.

Those around you can sense the invisible currents of purpose within you. Your thoughts have presence. *The Atmosphere You Permit Determines The Product You Produce.* Self-confidence creates a miraculous climate.

Solomon grew up with greatness. His own father was the greatest warrior Israel had ever known. His father's name was on the lips of thousands every day of his life. He was not a stranger to competent, articulate and powerful leaders.

Solomon was reared in the *House of the Uncommon*, which only served to enhance his sense of inferiority. When he became king, he had never fought a battle or written a book. Only his parents understood and discerned his destiny.

This positioned him for humility. He knew what he lacked. Many know they lack something, but few discover what it is. Unlike his father David, Solomon could not retrieve any memories of killing a bear and a lion. He had never killed a giant. But he had a secret weapon, and it was one that few men ever possess.

Solomon possessed the Weapon of Humility.

He had enough humility to recognize his limitations. He asked for Wisdom and strength. He pursued *supernatural* help, and it came. His confidence, faith and Wisdom became the talk of his generation.

7 Steps That Can Unlock Your Self-Confidence

1. Recognize That Your Creator Wants Good Things To Happen For You. James 1:17 says, "Every good gift and every perfect gift is from above, and cometh down from the Father of lights, with whom is no variableness, neither shadow of turning."

2. Make Certain That Your Dream Is Not Contrary To The Laws of God or Man. Your conscience must be at peace for your greatest ideas to emerge. You must not attempt to pursue anything that troubles your heart, soul and mind. The Seeds of Greatness grow best in the Soil of Peace and the name, *Solomon*, even means "peace."

3. Fill Every Conversation With Faith And Talk About Your Dream. Words matter. They *move* you toward your dream or away from it. Your words should continuously reflect hope in your future. When someone walks into your room with words of doubt and unbelief, boldly refute those words and *do not receive them.* Let others know clearly and confidently that great things are happening in your life. Remember, your faith is like a muscle that grows and becomes strong through continuous use.

4. Associate Often With Those Whose Fire Is Presently Burning Brighter Than Your Own. Pursue the greatness around you. Who are the most successful people you presently know? Who are the people who have succeeded in the same arena in which you desire to succeed? Schedule appointments with them. Treat them to a special lunch. Interrogate, interview and receive the information they have. Do not feel obligated to tell them all of your plans. Simply respect and humbly pursue their advice and counsel. Let them light your fire as often as possible.

5. Remember Your Own Dream Is A Special Seed You Are Sowing Into The Hearts of Others. Sometimes, they are excited and thrilled with you. However, there will be times when those closest to you are not *ready to receive.* A farmer knows his field requires preparation before he plants his Seed. Likewise, the minds and hearts of those you love may require preparation as well. Be patient.

6. Remember That Your Dream May Intimidate Those Closest To You And Make Them Feel Uncomfortable. It is important to understand that your dream is yours *alone.* Others do not *feel* what you feel, *see* what you see, or *know* what you know. How can they understand your joy when they have not lived with your sorrow? Yes, those closest to you may misread you or even misjudge you because they feel uncomfortable. You are forcing them to respond to your dream, and your enthusiasm may be intimidating. Perhaps they are "unstretched." You are excited about success, while they are hoping only to survive.

Several years ago, I got involved with a great organization. The young man I signed in the marketing plan was ecstatic. He caught the vision. It was a proven company where thousands had already done well, and he could hardly wait to get home and tell his family.

So a few days later I decided to call him and see how he was doing.

"I'm anxious to see you at the meeting tomorrow," I said enthusiastically.

"Uh, I don't think I'll be able to come," he said with discouragement in his voice.

"Of course, you will!" I countered.

"No, I talked to my family about my dream and goals. They laughed at me. They really don't believe this can happen." His hopes were dashed because he shared his dream with those who were *incapable of appreciating it.*

7. Keep Your Fire Fueled. Take the time to fertilize your own dreams. Talk about them. Build on them. Cover your walls with photographs and posters to help you visualize your dreams. You can't expect to light somebody else's fire until you have lit the fire within you.

What is your biggest dream at this moment? Are you willing to devote all your *time* and attention to it? Are you willing to create a *plan* that will make it happen? You see, the most wonderful thing that can happen to a dream is a specific plan of action. It births self-confidence.

4 Kinds of People Who Always Fail

The Undecided, Unlearned, Unfocused and Unexcited. The young man's very enthusiasm intimidated his family. Millions of people are living lives just that bland today.

The Saddest Tragedy of Life Is A Heart That Has Not Caught Fire. The mind of such a person is like a huge field into which no Seed has been sown. Nothing of worth is growing. This person will not produce greatness, miracles or an uncommon life. Learn to recognize this tragedy and stay focused, enthusiastic and aggressively happy.

Solomon was confident and became The Richest Man Who Ever Lived.

The Only Problem
In Your Life
Is A Wisdom Problem.

-MIKE MURDOCK

∽ 5 ∽

Solomon Acknowledged His Personal Limitations

Nobody Knows Everything.

Solomon recognized that he needed a power greater than his own. This was one of the most important and powerful secrets in his mind and life. Hear this incredible and powerful personal confession taken from 1 Kings 3:7, "I am but a little child: I know not how to go out or come in."

10 Facts You Should Know About Your Personal Limitations

1. **Everyone Has Weaknesses.** Some know their limitations, but few will acknowledge them.

2. **Admitting Weaknesses Contradicts Most Motivational Teaching Today.** This is in total contradiction with every motivational principle being taught in the business community today. In fact, motivational seminars on self-confidence are most often militant, bold and brash in teaching that you should never acknowledge that you "can't do it." Some instruct participants to pound their chests, yell out a personal cheer, or do something significant to point themselves

away from a weakness, problem or personal limitation. That's why they continue to fail.

3.   If You Do Not Acknowledge Limitations, You Will Not Seek Solutions For Them. When you ignore a personal weakness, it grows and multiplies. Don't deny your shortcomings. Facing them is the master key to overcoming them.

4.   Acknowledging Your Limitations Will Release An Unexplainable Energy Within You. You see, doing so immediately frees your mind to pursue the remedy and motivates others to assist you. It releases and energizes you. Solomon knew the principle and the power of internal integrity. Denying his weakness would have paralyzed him. Now, he has an antenna, attracting information, aid and encouragement from others.

5.   When You Admit A Weakness, You Activate Compassion In Others. On a recent trip to Georgia, my travel assistant realized that he was unfamiliar with the area. I suggested he stop. When I went into the service station to ask directions, everyone in the place got involved. In fact, they were happy and delighted to do so. I received far more instructions than I really found necessary. You see, *it is within the nature of man to help another.* It is normal and natural and something that God has placed inside of us. The moment everyone knew I needed help—the deepest part of them was activated to move toward me in caring, compassion and encouragement.

6.   When You Try To Do Everything Yourself, You Prevent Others From Moving Toward You. They feel unnecessary, insignificant and unimportant and you lose "the gold mine" within them.

Remember that arrogance is repelling. Pride moves people away from you, not toward you.

7. Something Inside of Others Longs To Become Necessary To You. If you are wise, you will permit others to participate in your dream and your life. They need it and you need it too. Have you ever felt the strings of your heart tug when your little boy said, "Daddy, I can't button my shirt. Will you help me?" Something inside you leaps forward and you drop everything you are doing to assist your child. Why? Because he needs you.

8. There Is Always Something You Are Not Discerning. Those close to you often see what you cannot see! That's why they are necessary to your life and the achieving of your dreams. This does not mean that your instincts and intuition are necessarily wrong, simply that they are sometimes limited, restricted and incomplete.

9. Others Can See Things You Do Not See. Something is hidden in everything around you. Something you cannot see, feel or know. That's why your opinions and conclusions are sometimes inaccurate. You can become so involved in achieving your dream that the pain, torment and wounds in others become hidden to you. You can become so obsessed with your goal that you fail to hear the cries and desires of others around you.

10. Uncommon Dreams Will Always Require The Observation of Others. Talk to those close to you and do not hesitate to ask them to tell you what they are seeing, hearing and discovering.

Acknowledge that there is a power greater than your own and that you need your Creator. In the religious world, many belief systems exist. To a thinking person, this can be troubling. Who was really right? Who knows the truth? There seems to be so many contradictions. Even when you read the Scriptures, you may come away with unanswered questions.

The *first step* to truth is to acknowledge any *wrong* you are aware of in your life.

The *second step* is to acknowledge your *need* for truth.

The *third step* is ask for and *pursue* truth continuously.

On page 45 of his book, *Well Done,* Dave Thomas, CEO of Wendy's International says, "Many people who come to me, especially since my work on behalf of adoption started, say they're going to remember me in their prayers, and, well, I take them seriously since I figure we all need as much help as we can get. I'm really thankful for people who pray for me."

Independence from your Creator will always birth a tragedy—usually, many tragedies.

Years ago my song writing generated hundreds of thousands of dollars. I placed the money in a special account and planned to live on the interest it created. I decided to live "independent" of everyone. Suddenly, an inner voice spoke into my conscience saying, *"Every step toward self-sufficiency is a step away from Me."* I froze. I sensed that I was wanting to live independent from the power above all powers, my Creator.

You see, *life was intended to be a faith experience.* It is the flow of faith that breathes energy, creativity and enthusiasm into everything you do.

Recently, a young teenage boy indicated that he

wanted to leave home. He despised chores and hated the restraint he was feeling from his parents.

"I am going to be independent from everyone. I trust no one and I will lean on no one. I will succeed alone," he boasted proudly.

"If you run away, how will you get to the airport?" I asked.

"Call a taxi," was his instant reply.

"Okay. Let me review this carefully with you," I said. "As you live your independent life from everyone else, you will reach for a telephone (owned by your father) and call an operator who will tell you the telephone number of the taxi. Then, the taxi driver will come here and take you to the airport. At the airport, you will hand the money to a ticket agent who will then process a ticket. Then you will have the pilot fly you to a city."

"How can you say your life is independent of everyone when you are asking everyone to participate in everything you are doing?" I asked.

He looked sheepishly. "I never thought of that."

Everything you are doing carries the imprint of others. Only a fool could fail to see that.

Solomon was The Richest Man Who Ever Lived.

He succeeded because he understood his personal limitations.

You can succeed significantly with your life.

You can have incredible friendships.

You can produce finances beyond your wildest imaginations.

But you will never do it alone. *Life is a collection of relationships,* and those relationships compensate for what you do not have.

As you pursue the dreams and goals of your life, take a sheet of paper and do what one of America's wealthiest men has suggested. Steven K. Scott, co-founder of the American Telecast Corporation, said in his book, *A Millionaire's Notebook,* "List what you consider your greatest weaknesses, both personally and professionally—lack of education, lack of career achievement, impatience, short temper, etc." Doing this will help you acknowledge your weaknesses, and *attract* those who are able to help you overcome them.

Solomon understood that you can only follow good advice when you recognize that you need it. This is one of the Golden Secrets that helped him become The Richest Man Who Ever Lived.

❧ 6 ❧

Solomon Boldly Announced His Dream To Others

➤◆◆

Your Dream Should Be Too Big To Contain.

This was the experience of Solomon. In 2 Chronicles 2:5, he says, "And the house which I build is great."

Your dream should be so big that it unleashes conversation around you.

This is important. Your dream must be big enough to consume you, or it will not move you. It must consume your time, your mind and your conversation.

Listen to Solomon's own words from 1 Kings 5:5, "And, behold, I purpose to build an house unto the name of the Lord my God, as the Lord spake unto David my father, saying, Thy son...shall build an house unto My name."

When you are in love, you tell everyone. You simply cannot keep it quiet. Your heart is on fire and excitement throbs within you. Every thought is about that person.

Telling others also destroys the option to fail.

One of the great explorers in the new world burned the boats after his arrival on shore to ensure that his fighting men would not run away from the challenge ahead.

You must do the same. If you whisper to yourself, "I'd better not tell anyone about my dream so I won't look stupid if I fail," you have just *created a bridge back to yesterday.* Stop building bridges to your past; it divides your attention and dilutes your energy and enthusiasm. You will be too busy considering yesterday to abandon yourself to your future.

Announce your dream boldly to others. It can make such a wonderful difference in your success. Are you somewhat embarrassed by your dream? Then *review it* again. Something is missing. Your dream should be something that *fuels the fire* within you. *It should make you want to wake up earlier* than everyone else and get started each day.

I wear a beautiful golden nugget bracelet engraved with the number of my desired weight. It keeps me *focused and excited.* When I look at it, I can see myself achieving my ideal weight. Yes, I have even told my family and staff about my desired goal.

What if I fail? I will not. But I have everything to gain by creating a climate of *expectation* around my life. It is often true that those who have no expectations of their own for their lives move toward the expectations of others.

It happened to Solomon's father. David announced to his brothers, King Saul, and the whole army, his intention to kill Goliath. He could not go back. He staked a claim with his words.

I really believe something remarkable happens in your life *when you seize a dream boldly*, confidently and with abandonment. Obstacles move out of your way. Those who might oppose you feel embarrassed. They are reluctant to stand and confront you.

When you announce your dream, doubters are forced to expose themselves or stand silent. *Either way, you are helped.* You see, when your announced goal or dream agitates your enemies, they will *reveal* themselves. This will *expose their strategies* and help you prepare for battle.

Noah announced that it was going to rain. He could not go back. His faith became focused. Doubt could no longer serve as a refuge. People were waiting to see if he was a true prophet. (Obviously, it is not necessary or even appropriate to announce *every part* of your plans. Some things require discretion and confidentiality.)

8 Miraculous Things Will Happen When You Boldly Announce Your Dream

1. Those Who Believe And Stand With You Will Be Energized And Encouraged. You have just given them a reason and a purpose to function in your world. Their Assignment is now clear and you have just released them from any options and potential alternatives.

2. Those Who Stand With You Will Suddenly Become Creative In Their Ideas For Assisting You. They will remember vendors, contacts and special business connections that are related to your dream. If you were to stay silent and not announce your goal, they would remain withdrawn and quiet in their own tiny world of mediocrity.

3. Those Who Are Tempted To Oppose You May Suddenly Weaken And Decide To Join You

When They See Your Determination. Boldness is magnetic. It changes a potential obstacle into a bridge of opportunity. Those Who Are Weak Often Become Strong In The Presence of The Bold. Your declaration allows them to tap into an invisible reservoir of energy, enthusiasm and purpose that lies dormant within them.

4. **Those Who Might Disagree With You Privately Are Forced To Expose Themselves To You Publicly.** Their countenance will send a message. If they have privately opposed you, your public declaration will require them to respond publicly before the faces of those they have poisoned. At that point, they may give you all the reasons you cannot succeed. This helps you, because as my dear friend Sherman Owens teaches—*Unhappy Voices Always Provide Uncommon Ideas.*

5. **When You Announce Your Dream Boldly, You Make It More Difficult To Fail.** Your declaration removes your option to go backward, leaving you free to abandon yourself to methods that can succeed. An incredible flow of energy, enthusiasm, and ideas are then released toward your new dream. *Your heart and spirit are energized.* No one can really explain it. Words are so powerful, but those who practice the martial arts know that even the chants of the crowd can affect a fighter in the ring.

6. **When You Boldly Announce Your Dream, You Instantly Create A Golden Connection, A Common Denominator, For Every Person Who Has Wanted To Accomplish Such A Dream.** Others will be happy to assist you because you have linked everyone instantly to one common goal.

7.   When You Boldly Announce Your Dream, You Instantly Expose Your Enemies. When they see your boldness, they will move swiftly to stop you. This always gives you an advantage because *An Enemy Exposed Can Become An Enemy Defeated.*   An unexposed enemy is far more dangerous to you.

8.   When You Boldly Announce Your Dreams, Non-Essential Tasks That Do Not Help You Achieve That Dream Are Exposed And Can Be Eliminated. Those around you must know your priorities.   Otherwise, you will pick up hundreds of small burdens along the way that have nothing to do with the achievement of your dream. *The sooner they are exposed, the sooner they can be eliminated.*

In Genesis 37 through 41, we read that Joseph experienced this when he announced his dream to his brothers. They immediately turned on him. It might appear that he made a mistake. But in the long-term, the hatred of his brothers moved him quickly into the land of Egypt where, in a few short years, his power and influence were surpassed only by that of the Pharaoh.

Miraculous things occur when you take decisive action and boldly announce your dreams. Solomon knew this. It is one of the Golden Secrets that helped Solomon become The Richest Man Who Ever Lived.

An Uncommon Future
Requires An
Uncommon Mentor.

-MIKE MURDOCK

≈ 7 ≈

SOLOMON CONSULTED OTHER UNCOMMON ACHIEVERS

Someone Close To You Contains Answers.
Solomon recognized this. He documented his pursuit of a major king who held the keys to his dream—the building of the Temple. In 2 Chronicles 2:3, we read that "Solomon sent to Huram, the king of Tyre, saying, As thou didst deal with David my father, and didst send him cedars to build him an house to build therein, even so deal with me."

10 Qualities of Uncommon Achievers

1. Uncommon Achievers Always Consult Others. On page 59 of his book, *It Ain't As Easy As It Looks,* one of Ted Turner's close friends, Irwin Mazo, says, "Ted got good advice in those days, and he generally followed it."

2. Uncommon Achievers Will Invest Whatever Is Necessary To Learn The Secrets of Others. A few years ago I was browsing through a bookstore with my travel assistant. He could not help but express his shock when I purchased a book for $84.00.

"Why would you spend $84.00 on one book?" was his incredulous question.

"Son, I am not just buying a book, I am paying for the author's research and experience. I will learn in two hours what took him twenty years to discover. Paying $84.00 for twenty years research and experience makes this one of the most inexpensive investments I will ever make."

I have read that 80 percent of Americans will never purchase a book after the age of eighteen and only seven out of a hundred religious people have ever walked into a religious bookstore.

3.   Uncommon Achievers Treasure Every Moment They Are In The Presence of Greatness. When you are in the presence of greatness, drop your pail in their well! You may never get a second opportunity. When you talk to a lawyer, ask him the three most important things you should know about legal matters. When you are in the presence of a great doctor, ask him the three common mistakes people make regarding their health. When you are in the presence of an effective mother, ask her the keys to unlocking greatness in a small child. *Greatness surrounds you like winds every day.* Your responsibility is to harness it, pull it toward you and absorb it.

4.   Uncommon Achievers Pursue Other Uncommon Achievers. Who has done what you want to do? Who has had remarkable success? Do you desire to be successful in the real estate business? Locate the top three realtors within a 200-mile radius of your home. Schedule appointments with them. Take your microcassette recorder and legal pad with you, and ask them to tell you what important questions you should be asking!

Recently, a young man said to me, "I don't know the questions to ask you!"

"Then ask me to give you a list of the questions that are important!" I replied.

Life is so simple. *We are stumbling over pebbles instead of climbing mountains.*

5.   Uncommon Achievers Conduct Themselves Wisely In The Presence of Greatness. Protocol matters.   How you conduct yourself may determine whether you ever receive a second invitation. The Bible has a great deal to say about protocol and conduct in the presence of uncommon people. Queen Esther recognized this when she meditated and thought deeply on approaching the king regarding the assassination efforts of Haman, the friend of the king. Joseph shaved himself and changed his clothes to create a climate of acceptance when approaching Pharaoh with the interpretation of his dream. Naomi advised Ruth to wash the barley out of her hair, and change her clothes before approaching the wealthy landowner, Boaz.

6.   Uncommon Achievers Have Uncommon Expectations of Others. You cannot saunter and amble into their presence as if they are average.

7.   Uncommon Achievers Are Aware of Their Own Uncommon Qualities. They may not respond instantly. You may never even discern their true opinion of you.

8.   Uncommon Achievers Study Carefully Everything That Comes Close To Them. They evaluate its potential danger or potential benefit and reward. They see everything close to them as a hurdle or a help; a bridge or a barricade; a pit or a passage; a problem or a solution; a door or a wall. You must qualify for continued access to them.

9. Uncommon Achievers Often Discern Your True Motive And Attitude Before You Ever Open Your Mouth. They have uncommon intuition and instincts. They can read your heart a mile away because their experiences have exposed them to cunning, shrewd and deceptive people. Their instincts are like radar. When you come into their presence, do not attempt to be shrewd or cunning or try to outwit them. Make no attempt to impress them. Become a learner instead.

10. Uncommon Achievers Reward Those Who Truly Respect Them With Continued Access.

4 Protocol Rules For Appointments With Uncommon Achievers

1. Do Not Take Them On A Journey Into Your Past Exploits. The best way to impress someone is not to try. If requested, brief them with a concise explanation and summary of your life. This can and should be done in less than thirty seconds. They are not interested in how great you are. They have a schedule to keep. Respect their focus.

2. Familiarize Yourself With Their Achievements Before Your Appointment. For example, if you want to meet with a legendary lawyer—familiarize yourself with the top three cases of his career. Review his books and develop an understanding of his philosophy toward life. Many years ago, a television talk show host wanted to meet with me. The pastor at the church in which I was speaking persisted. So I took off the entire afternoon and went over to the TV station. As we began to talk, she seemed startled to learn that I was a musician. "Oh, you write songs, too?" she asked. I was stunned. I've written more than 5,000 songs. Some are known around the world. Why was I sitting there wasting an entire afternoon discussing my life with someone so unconcerned that she did not even prepare for the interview? I closed the conversation quickly and made a decision. Never again will I allow someone to interview me who has not read my books and shown respect for my calling. My time is too precious to me.

3. When You Talk To An Uncommon Achiever, Discuss Their Focus, Not Your Own.

4. Be Honest, Open And Sincere About What You Want And Expect From The Appointment. Do not "circle the airport" with words. Go ahead and "land the plane!" When someone tells me they need to talk to me for more than five minutes, I know they probably have no idea what questions they want to ask. I personally believe that 90 percent of conversations could be shortened to five minutes without any loss whatsoever.

Solomon consulted other uncommon achievers about his dream. This is one of the Golden Secrets which helped him become The Richest Man Who Ever Lived.

What You Are Hearing
Is Creating
What You Are Feeling.

-MIKE MURDOCK

☜ 8 ☞

SOLOMON LOVED PEOPLE ENOUGH TO INVOLVE THEM IN HIS DREAM AND FUTURE

Never Underestimate The Importance of People.

We live in a busy, hurried world and it is easy to get caught up in the whirlwind of busyness, tasks and goals. But Solomon knew that you will never achieve a significant dream without the involvement of others.

Solomon fully grasped the wonder of humanity. In 1 Kings 3:9, we read that Solomon pleaded with God for special and extraordinary Wisdom, "Give therefore Thy servant an understanding heart to judge Thy people, that I may discern between good and bad: for who is able to judge this Thy *so great a people?*"

Solomon saw the hidden treasure in others around him in a way that no one had seen it before. He regarded the people around him as more than servants and employees. He saw them as more than sources of revenue and taxes. His love ran deep enough to ask God for uncommon ability to bless and strengthen those he governed.

Solomon was not afraid to ask others to get involved with the dream of his lifetime. A young man approached me after a speaking engagement one evening. He was shy and hesitant. He wanted to involve me in a business idea he had, but he was never quite able to tell me his intention. After he walked away, I thought, "He will never achieve his goal until it becomes more important than anything else in his life."

Asking is the first step toward receiving.

26 Powerful Facts Uncommon Achievers Know About People

1.   **You Will Always Need People.**
2.   **Success Is A Collection of Relationships.** Without clients, a lawyer has no career. Without patients, a doctor has no future. Without composers, a singer has nothing to sing. Your future is connected to people. Your success is dependent upon people.
3.   **Greatness Is All Around You.** You must look for it. Expect it. Celebrate it. Pursue it, and reward it wherever it is found.
4.   **The Master Key To Achieving Anything Significant Is Inspiring Those Around You To Commit To Your Vision Until It Becomes Their Vision As Well.**
5.   **Everyone Will Have Something Different To Impart Into Your Life.** Remember—someone close to you needs something you possess. Likewise, someone else possesses something you need to achieve your dreams and goals as well. Each person around you possesses a different "body of knowledge." It is your personal responsibility to drop your pail in their well and draw it out. As Proverbs 11:14 teaches, "Where no counsel is, the people fall: but in the multitude of

counsellors there is safety." Some of the people around you are logical, and some are analytical. Others will be creative and energizing, but the contribution of *each* person is vital.

6. **You Must Be Willing To Listen To Others.** We all see through different eyes, feel with different hearts and hear with different ears.

7. **Someone Close To You Knows Something That You Must Know or You Will Not Succeed.** Stop. When someone tries to tell you something, take the time to hear them out. One piece of information can sometimes mean the difference between success and failure. The quality of your decisions depends on your ability to listen.

8. **You Must Deposit Your Best Efforts Into Others.** Solomon believed that those around him deserved his best efforts. That is why he prayed for uncommon Wisdom to aid and guide them. He felt a personal responsibility to improve the quality of their lives. In 1 Kings 3:8, Solomon called the people around him "a great people."

9. **You Must Be Willing To Reach Out To People.** Solomon was humble. His first request to his Creator was for personal assistance to help those around him become successful. The arrogant never reach out. They attempt everything alone.

10. **You Must Love People Enough To Empty Your Life Into Them.**

11. **You Must Love People Enough To Pursue Ways To Benefit And Reward Them.**

12. **You Must Love People Enough To Prepare And Be Changed So They Can Succeed Because of You.**

13. You Must Celebrate The Differences In People. Solomon networked with many cultures. (He was the leader of the commerce of his day, and the first to send ships to other countries.) Many never celebrate the fact that we are all different. People often fear those they do not understand. Then they withdraw, criticize and cast aside.

14. Discern The Dominant Gift God Has Deposited In Others Just For You. Many years ago, I hired a vibrant and energized young lady to run my music company. Everyone loved her and considered her a delight. Since I traveled a great deal, I was often out of the office and unable to oversee her work. When I finally found an opportunity to look over her files, I was dismayed to find that she was not organized in any way. My financial documents were a mess. Envelopes were mislabeled, and bank statements were in disarray. I was horrified.

I called her into my office and gently explained, "I really love you and appreciate the joy that you bring into this office. But, I will have to fire you."

After she left, I noticed an unexplainable emptiness in the atmosphere at my office. The staff had lost its energy and excitement.

I now realize that this young woman had the nature of a *cheerleader,* rather than the mentality of a coach. *Spontaneity was her gift to me.* Structure was not. If I could do it over again, I would simply place her in a different position. Her countenance, energy and desire to be hospitable were too rare. She was the spark plug of my whole staff.

Marriages often fragment because people fail to understand this principle. Husbands pressure wives to change. Wives pressure husbands to change. Variety creates intrigue. Unpredictability has its rewards. Structure has its own product.

15. Remember That People Need To Hear Your Good Thoughts About Them. Solomon celebrated people—everywhere he found them. First Kings 10:8 says, "Happy are thy men, happy are these thy servants, which stand continually before thee, and that hear thy Wisdom." *What You Are Hearing Is Creating What You Are Feeling.*

16. People Around You Possess The Solutions To Your Problems. Solomon asked everybody to help him.

17. Involve As Many People As Possible In Your Dream. You need people to assist you in order to achieve your dream. Solomon wrote and reached out to many to assist him in the building of the incredible Temple.

He listened to *people.*

He listened to *kings.*

He listened to *leaders.*

He even listened to two quarreling harlots.

He listened to *enthusiastic* voices for *encouragement* wherever he found them.

18. Even Unhappy People Can Birth Incredible Ideas For You. Solomon listened to *unhappy* voices for *ideas. He inspired the gifted to assist him.* In 2 Chronicles 2:7, we read Solomon's words, "Send me now therefore a man cunning to work in gold, and in silver, and in brass, and in iron, and in purple, and crimson, and blue, and that can skill to grave with the cunning men that are with me in Judah and in Jerusalem, whom David my father did provide."

Solomon respected the skill of others. He *searched* them out, *rewarded* them and *paid* them well.

19. Uncommon Achievers Notice Quality People. Donald Trump, the billionaire from New York said, "I'm just looking to hire the best talent wherever I can find it." Many years ago, I read that one of the master secrets of Dr. Oral Roberts, the founder of Oral Roberts University, was that he literally combed the earth looking for the most highly qualified people to surround him.

20. You Will Only Succeed In Life To The Degree You Succeed With People. Are you having difficulty in your relationships with others? Do your fellow workers resent you? Why? Do those who work under you long to work under another manager in another department? Be honest with yourself.

21. Everyone Has Something Different To Give.

22. Some Friendships Are For Encouragement. Their words compliment and edify. They admire your labor and achievements and exude enthusiasm when you achieve a goal. Their excitement energizes you.

23. Some Friends Analyze And Critique You. These types are also necessary. They are not always enthusiastic and encouraging, but their scrutiny prevents tragic consequences and wrong decisions.

24. Some Friends Energize You. When these friends are around, you want to achieve your greatest dreams and goals. In their presence, you make huge plans and throw caution to the wind. You become a risk-taker. You see the potential and possibility in everything. These kinds of friends are an important key to unlocking your *faith.*

Solomon was brilliant. He realized every person sees something different. When he surrounded himself with their expertise, opinions and viewpoints, they imparted and deposited into him *their* Wisdom. He became a melting pot of understanding.

It is true that every person is not necessarily "your kind of person." You may not feel comfortable with everyone. You may not always be energized by their presence. But every person has a valuable deposit to make into your life when you truly understand the need for it.

25. You Will Need Many Kinds of Personalities Involved In Your Life. Each will enlarge, educate and strengthen you. Some offer spontaneity and freedom of expression.

The unwise limit themselves.

The wise accept the impartation of many.

In Proverbs 11:14, it is written: "In the multitude of counsellors there is safety."

26. Relationship Skills Can Be Learned. This will take time and require focus. Most of all, it will mean being totally honest. Ask your supervisor for suggestions regarding books, seminars or personal evaluation. Be willing to be corrected. When you offend, be swift to apologize, and show a sincere desire to develop and be changed.

7 Keys In Getting Along With People

1. Stop Focusing On The Flaws of People And "Catch Them Doing Something Right."

2. Praise Others Publicly And Privately.

3. Recognize Completed Tasks, Good Attitudes, And Be Swift To Reward Those Who Assist You In Achieving Your Goal.

4. Do Not Permit Bitter Feelings To Fester And Grow Within You. Do not advertise your conflicts with everyone else. Rather, approach the person who has offended you, directly and in private. Make things right.

5. Remember Dialogue Always Births Miraculous Changes.

6. Recognize That Words Are The "Golden Bridges" From The Pit To The Palace.

7. Fall In Love With People And People Will Fall In Love With You. Someone has said, "People do not care how important you are, it is important to them that you really care." Someone else said, "People wear huge, invisible signs around their necks that say— Please tell me I am important to you." (I think it was Mary Kay Ash who said this.) Remembering this simple key can make a profound difference.

The countenance of those near you may look stoic, uncommitted and uninspired. But, within every human heart beats a fervent desire to be needed, desired and celebrated. Do not stress to others how easily you could live without them—remind them how much their presence has improved your life.

The Master Secret hidden inside the bosom of Solomon is found in his description of his people. He called them "a great people."

> ▶ Those around you are great. Become worthy of them.

> ▶ Those around you can *become* great. Become their "bridge to greatness."

▶ Uncommon achievers *recognize and reward* other uncommon achievers.

Loving people is one of the Golden Secrets that helped Solomon become The Richest Man Who Ever Lived.

A Short Pencil
Is Better
Than A Long Memory.

-MIKE MURDOCK

≈ 9 ≈

SOLOMON CLEARLY EXPLAINED HIS EXPECTATIONS OF OTHERS TO THEM

Always Document Your Expectations.
He carefully sculptured a plan. He delegated responsibilities. He knew which tasks to assign to those around him. This greatly decreased their stress.

Solomon explained his expectations to other leaders. He wrote to Hiram, King of Tyre, in 1 Kings 5:6, "Now therefore command thou that they hew me cedar trees out of Lebanon; and my servants shall be with thy servants: and unto thee will I give hire for thy servants according to all that thou shalt appoint: for thou knowest that there is not among us any that can skill to hew timber like unto the Sidonians."

You must *explain fully your expectations of others to them.* Do they have before them a written contract or job description that makes it easy for them to review and stay focused? Is it in *writing?* Verbal instructions can be distorted, misinterpreted and forgotten.

Solomon documented with great precision exactly what he wanted others to do. This removed doubt and uncertainty. It released them to abandon themselves to their Assignment.

Recently, I discussed this in great detail with a wonderful and competent man. He was brilliant. His desk was orderly, but those around him seemed very flustered, which bewildered and puzzled him. As we began to talk, I made some interesting discoveries.

He really expected others to *read* his mind.

He expected others to have his *energy*.

He was unaware of the continuous distractions and interruptions his staff experienced on a daily basis. He had withdrawn from the public flow of traffic and people and left his staff to face them for him. He had become detached, alienated and distant. In his own little world, he was king. However, all those around him were in confusion because he had not given them precise instructions regarding his expectations and the deadlines he had imposed.

Dictation is one of the master secrets to uncommon achievement. (You can talk four to six times faster than you can write.)

I travel a lot. So it became commonplace for me to give verbal instructions by phone on a daily basis. I soon became frustrated because I would return from trips to find that many of the assignments I had given my staff had not been completed on time and in an effective manner.

When I began to *dictate* the instructions and provide my staff with a typed list of my personal expectations, the percentage of completed tasks was astounding. Why? Because I was providing a clear-cut job description. They could look and analyze. They could ask questions. They could review and retrieve information.

This explains the disorganized and stressful home life of many families. It is rare to walk into a teenager's room and see a written list of instructions on the bulletin board. Mom is screaming at the top of her voice at the other end of the house. Dad sits by the fireplace, staring vacantly at the newspaper trying to shut out the turmoil. In many cases, clearly defined chores would remove a lot of the stress instantly. The uncertainty and the lack of understanding causes us to misjudge and misinterpret each other.

I walked through a huge plant several years ago in Pennsylvania. The wealthy owner was a short, abrupt and energetic man. When I asked the secret of his success, his son spoke up.

"Daddy always says to make something so simple that the biggest dummy in the world could understand it."

This man spelled out everything. Every bulletin board had big, bold, simple explanations of laws and rules and expectations. No small print. No legalese.

He made it easy for others to understand his expectations.

Invest in a special meeting with those around you. Ask them questions and make certain that they understand beyond a shadow of a doubt what their *daily* tasks are to be. What their *weekly* tasks are to be. What *monthly* reports are they responsible for? Write it out so clearly that it can never be doubted or mishandled again.

If there is one thing I have discovered, it is the profound and consistent ability of those around you to misinterpret and forget everything you have said to them. I cannot recall a week that I have not had to repeat something over again that has been established for years.

▶ People must *see* your expectations in *writing.*
▶ People must *keep seeing* your expectations in writing.
▶ People must *be reminded* to keep looking at what you wrote!

Never underestimate the ability of the human mind to forget. *Never.*

Why doesn't everyone document, delegate and follow through on tasks they give to others? Because it is time-consuming and exhausting. It slows you down and keeps you from those things that excite you more. When you invest the time to help others fully understand their roles and the rewards for completing those tasks, however, your own life will leap forward exhilarated and enthused.

When do you want lunch? Every day? What are the top ten lunches on the menu that you have approved? Donald Trump has one person whose sole function is to keep his life *organized.* Who has that responsibility in your life? Who approves the purchase orders in your office? What are the criteria and guidelines for *approving* them? *Who* is responsible for the *vehicle* maintenance at your home? What is the *schedule* for consistent trips to the garage?

Solomon assumed nothing.

He communicated *constantly.*

He communicated *publicly.*

He *documented* his desires.

Solomon clearly explained to others *his expectations of them.* That is one of the Golden Secrets that caused him to become The Richest Man Who Ever Lived.

≈ 10 ≈

SOLOMON DOCUMENTED AND DEVELOPED A PLAN FOR ACHIEVING HIS GOALS

───────◆───────

Your Plan Is The Map of Your Intentions.

Solomon was specific and detailed when he planned the temple—his $500 billion dream. You can read 1 Kings for a detailed description of Solomon's plan, which includes this passage, "And the house which king Solomon built for the Lord, the length thereof was threescore cubits, and the breadth thereof twenty cubits, and the height thereof thirty cubits." Solomon was meticulous.

But this book involves more than Solomon. It involves you. I urge you to focus on your dream and develop a plan for achieving it.

6 Facts You Should Know About Planning

1. **Planning Is A Written Picture of Your Journey To Your Goal.** It takes time. It takes reworking. But it is the secret of champions.

2. **Planning Helps Eliminate Wrong People From Your Schedule.** One of the most successful lawyers in America invests the first hour of every day in carefully planning that day. He believes that quality

time should be invested in *qualifying* those who deserve an appointment with him.

3. Planning Focuses Your Attention On Where It Is Needed Most. Mary Kay Ash was one of the most successful women of America, worth more than $300 million. She said that every morning she invested time in creating a plan. She chose six tasks she would accomplish each day. She worked Task One as far as she can move it. Then she worked on Task Two. She never worked on Task Six, until she had finished everything she could do on the first five.

4. Planning Requires Discipline And Determination Whether You Feel Like It or Not. Planning is often wearisome. Sometimes you will be tempted to think, "It would be a lot quicker to go ahead and *begin* my work rather than trying to lay out a plan." Avoid the trap of an unplanned day.

5. Planning Will Always Reveal The Shortest Route To Your Goal. It focuses your total attention on the *people* necessary, the available *time*, and the *financial costs* involved.

Planning Time Is Never, Never, Never Wasted Time!

What is causing you to avoid planning? Some avoid it because they like spontaneity, the freedom of doing what they feel like doing when they feel like doing it. Unfortunately, this kind of behavior ignores the existence of obstacles, unexpected problems and unclear instructions. It is an open invitation to problems. Would you drive an hour to a restaurant without calling ahead to make certain it was open? Of course not. Would you go Christmas shopping without making certain you had your checkbook or cash with you? Of course not.

6.   Planning Is Simply Thinking Ahead On Paper. Create your personal dream list and call it, "My Lifetime Goals and Dreams." Now, dream with wild and unrestrained abandonment and enthusiasm for the next five minutes. Imagine that the pen in your hand is a "Golden Miracle Wand." Just suppose it was handed to you by your Creator and He said, *"Anything you write on this Dream List will occur during your lifetime.* Regardless of how miraculous or wonderful it is, I will make it come true if you simply write it down."

Think about it.

Wouldn't that be wonderful and incredibly exciting? Of course it would!

So do it. Write quickly and freely, and never edit your dreams. Stop thinking, "Well, I really could do without this" or "I don't know if my mate or parents would really agree that this is a worthy goal or dream."

Those things don't really matter right now.

Your most immediate Assignment is to document your dreams. Write down everything that you could desire, dream or want during your entire lifetime.

Here are a few ideas to help get you started.

▶ Would you like to learn a foreign language?

▶ Would you like to write your own book? If so, what is it about?

▶ What country would you like to visit?

▶ Is there a special person you would like to meet?

▶ Is there a specific business opportunity you keep seeing in your imagination every day?

▶ What is the most beautiful car you can imagine owning? If you could have it next year, *describe it fully on your dream list today.*

▶ Would you like to be *debt-free?* What needs to happen for that to occur within the next five years?

▶ Do you hate being *overweight?* What would be your desired weight if you could simply wave your pencil and it would occur instantly? Write it down.

Do not edit these dreams or prejudge their worth. *Simply write them down.* Do not delete or eliminate anything that comes to your mind. You have an entire lifetime to make any changes! Right now, your goal is to create the most marvelous Dream List you could possibly imagine for the next five minutes. Now, do this before you continue!

7 Steps In Organizing Your Dream

1.   **List The Single Greatest Goal You Want To Achieve With Your Life.**

2.   **List Five Reasons Why You Want To Achieve It.** Who will benefit because of your goal and dream? This is very important. In difficult times, you will need to remind yourself of what motivated you to do it in the beginning!

3.   **Take A Sheet of Paper And Write Down Everything That You Can Imagine That Might Be Involved In Achieving This Dream.** Every step, every detail you can think of. It might be even easier to dictate it. (Remember, you can talk four to six times faster than you can write!)

4.   **List The Potential Problems That Exist And Note The Current Solutions Obvious To You.**

5.   **List The Names of Everyone You Could Possibly Involve In Your Dream.**

6.   Create Your Personal "Circle of Counsel" For Your Dream. These individuals will serve as your advisors, brainstorming and sharing with you regarding your goal and dream. They will help *define* and *refine* your dream and plan.

7.   Define Your Personal Rewards For Achieving This Goal. Be honest and write out any financial, emotional or physical rewards your goals will create.

Solomon believed in planning. It is one of the Golden Secrets that helped him become The Richest Man Who Ever Lived.

The Currency
of Life On Earth
Is Time.

-MIKE MURDOCK

≈ 11 ≈

SOLOMON KEPT A
DETAILED SCHEDULE

Time Always Matters To The Wealthy.

The only real gift you have been given by life is the gift of Time. You received Time as the currency of this earth. When you saw a friendship you desired, you sowed Time into it and produced a relationship.

You had no money. But you met an employer with money who wanted your Time instead. You traded your Time for his money. That became your profession and source of income.

You wanted a healthy body. So you used Time as currency and sowed it into exercise, producing a healthier body.

Japan has the Yen. England has the Pound. France has the Franc. Germany has the Mark. Italy has the Lire. Mexico has the Peso. The United States has the Dollar.

The Currency of Life On Earth Is Time.

I have studied the lives of many successful men and women. The major difference I have seen between the poor and the powerful, the unemployed and the employed, the successful and the failing, the impoverished and the rich, is *their opinion of Time.*

I have not met a poor person who was consciously aware of Time. I have yet to meet a wealthy person who was *not* consciously aware of Time.

Solomon understood the principle of using Time as *currency*. Listen to this meticulous documentation in 1 Kings 6:1, "And it came to pass in the four hundred and eightieth year after the children of Israel were come out of the land of Egypt, in the fourth year of Solomon's reign over Israel, in the month of Zif, which is the second month, that he began to build the house of the Lord."

► Solomon knew *what* he intended to achieve.
► Solomon knew *when* he intended to achieve it.

Time is a mysterious thing. Yet it is the most sacred gift you have ever received from your Creator.

► Whatever you have today, you traded *Time* for it.
► Whatever you do not have or own, you have been *unwilling* to trade your time for.

Everything is a trade-off. *Everything.*

"I could make double pay," said a friend to me recently. "But it would require me to be away from my family two weeks each month. I have decided to stay in my present position, keep my present salary, so that I can be home each evening with my children when they come from school." My friend consciously traded an increased salary for something he desired more than money—Time with his family.

You must decide how important Time is to you.

A few days ago, someone said to me, "I want to come to your house and spend a couple of days just knocking around talking. When will you be home?"

I laughed. What a joke! "I don't 'knock around,'" I answered. There is not a day in my life that I do not schedule something that matters. I keep my schedule and I am always *moving* toward my future.

"Meet me for a cup of coffee," was a recent request from a flippant young man. I thought for a moment. But it did not take long to come to a decision. My staff, television programs and various responsibilities require over $1,000 an hour, eight hours a day during our work week. Lingering over that cup of coffee for one hour would actually cost me $1,000...*of my time.* Was it worth it? I analyzed the results of that anticipated conversation at the restaurant. I determined that it would fall way short of $1,000 in value. I did not want to appear harsh or uncaring, but I could not think of anything worthwhile we would discuss. This person was neither pursuing my Wisdom, nor interested in imparting Wisdom to me! While others may qualify for leisure time, it is important to know the difference.

4 Important Keys That Will Help You Keep A Productive Schedule

1. Picture Clearly What You Want To Accomplish As A Goal or A Dream. Picture what you want to accomplish on that day. Break it down into small increments. Treat each hour as an employee or associate. Give each hour an Assignment. Spell that Assignment out clearly.

2. Prioritize And List Each of These Things To Do In The Order of Their Importance. As I said earlier, Mary Kay Ash said this was one of the most important keys of her life. Every morning, she wrote down six goals she wanted to complete that day. She worked on number one until she was finished or went as far as she could. That was a major key in her life.

Few people schedule a day well. And yet, today is the life you are living. Yesterday Is In The Tomb, And Tomorrow Is In The Womb. Yesterday is dead and tomorrow is not yet born.

In one sense, *the only place you will ever be is today.* You do not really have a future. When you get there—you will call it *today!*

3. Keep Your Appointments Focused And Limited. If someone asks you for a 9:00 appointment, make it "9:00 to 9:20 a.m." Always establish a time to conclude the appointment. *Always.* This means that if the person is ten minutes late, you must say, "I'm so sorry. I only have ten minutes left to meet with you today." This helps them to become consciously aware of your time.

4. Always Keep Moving Even When Things Around You Hit A Lull. Reach for the telephone and make that important call you have not had time to make. Pull out some notes and document them, but keep things moving.

Keeping a detailed schedule is one of the Golden Secrets that helped Solomon become The Richest Man Who Ever Lived.

≈ 12 ≈

SOLOMON NEGOTIATED EVERYTHING

Uncommon Negotiation Creates Uncommon Rewards.

Negotiation is getting something you *want* by helping others get what they want or *need.* Someone has said, "You do not get in life what you deserve—you get what you negotiate for."

Solomon was a master negotiator. He dialogued and kept the lines of communication open. He was a genius networker. He negotiated royal trade routes. He negotiated with his builders. And he constantly negotiated with Hiram, the king of Tyre.

Because of his skill as a negotiator, Solomon's empire became the crossroads between nations. In 1 Kings 10:28-29, we learn that Egypt needed horses and Silicia had plenty of them. Yet the two were bitter enemies. Because he grasped the immeasurable influence of negotiation, Solomon became the bridge between the two nations.

Study the lives of extraordinary and uncommon achievers. They accept nothing at face value. Instead, they analyze and scrutinize. They evaluate each situation and then make ridiculous offers to bring the price down.

Uncommon men are uncommon *negotiators.*

On page 51 of his book, *The Art of the Deal,* Donald Trump says about his father, "He'd negotiate just as hard with the supplier of mops and floor wax as he would with the general contractor for the larger items on a project."

9 Success Keys That Will Help You Negotiate For What You Want When Dealing With A Person, Company or Vendor

1.   Find Out Everything You Can Possibly Know About That Company or Person or Product. Information is strength. You cannot make appropriate decisions without current, accurate data. You should know all essential information before a crisis arises.

2.   Do Not Hurry.   Uncommon negotiators move carefully. Once they understand what they are willing to invest, they carefully build their case for a long-term quality decision. There is an old saying, "The one who hurries loses." Lamentations 3:25 gives us an important Wisdom Principle, "The Lord is good unto them that wait for Him."

3.   Find Out What The Other Person Needs The Most. When you are negotiating with someone, things are never as they first appear. It may seem that someone needs money when he or she is really desperately needing more time. People are rarely angry for the reasons they tell you, and they are rarely anxious to sell something for the reasons they indicate. Take time to dialogue and listen.

4.   Remember The Greatest Weapon At The

Negotiating Table Is The Ability To Listen. The person who listens the most, with sincerity and purity of heart, will always gather the data needed to make a quality decision.

The person who talks the least has the most to gain. Why? You never have to explain what you do not say. You never have to retract, alter or correct a statement or observation. Permit others to open their hearts and share.

5. The One Who Asks The Most Questions Controls The Conversation. Questions determine the flow of answers. Therefore, you will not receive answers unless you ask the appropriate questions. Write the questions down. Meditate on them and analyze them. As your questions are answered, write the answers down also.

6. When In Doubt, Always Tape Record The Negotiations. This helps you to recall facts that you might otherwise easily forget. It is often possible to listen to the recorded conversation and hear something that you missed the first time due to the pressure of the moment.

7. Never Make A Major Decision When You Are Tired. One of the great American presidents refused to make decisions after 3:00 in the afternoon. Tired eyes rarely see a good future. Take time to rest, relax and rejuvenate yourself.

8. Negotiate For Long-Term Results Instead of Immediate Results. Solomon made decisions that lasted for many years. He was known for his rule of peace. Within forty years, he had created a network of commerce unparalleled in his day. One of the greatest secrets of his riches is that he refused to make a decision for an immediate profit alone. He was a long-term thinker.

I have often thought of Sam Walton, who refused to invest in any company based on short-term profit. He always wanted to know where the company would be in ten years. Some Japanese companies have 100-year plans. They think *long-term.*

Stop for a moment. Where do you want your company to be twenty years from today? Now, formulate a plan toward that desired end. This will help you enjoy the journey more than you ever dreamed because planning takes the stress off the present. It births patience and hope and attracts serious investors into your life.

9. Never Appear Desperate To Close A Deal. When vultures discern weakness, they move in to finish the kill on a victim. On page 37 of his book, *The Art of the Deal,* Donald Trump, one of the most effective negotiators in America today, says, "The worst thing you can possibly do in a deal is to seem desperate to make it. That makes the other guy smell blood, and then you're dead. The best thing you can do is deal from strength, and leverage is the biggest strength you can have."

Solomon was an uncommon negotiator. That is one of the Golden Secrets that helped him to become The Richest Man Who Ever Lived.

≈ 13 ≈

SOLOMON ALWAYS LISTENED TO BOTH SIDES BEFORE MAKING A DECISION

No One Tells You Everything.
There is always something that you do not know.
You must keep listening, in order to *hear.*
You must keep listening, in order to *know.*
You must keep listening, in order to make a *quality* decision.

Solomon never hurried in his decision-making. He did not rush to his conclusions. He knew that everybody had a story to tell and his responsibility was to hear it—*both sides of it.* Two prostitutes came to him. He did not kill them. He did not merely ban them from the country. Instead, he listened to their pain. His conduct toward unholy, unwise people increased his fame and brought him great honor.

Listening Is Your Gift To Others.
It is usually the most appreciated gift you can give. When someone is hurting, your greatest contribution to them is to listen. Proverbs 18:13 says, "He that answereth a matter before he heareth it, it is folly and shame unto him."

Proverbs 1:5 says, "A wise man will hear."

5 Secrets Solomon Used In Listening To Others

1.   **He Listened...For Details.** Some were left out. Some were overemphasized.
2.   **He Listened For Pain.**
3.   **He Listened For Envy And Jealousy.**
4.   **He Listened For Discrepancy And Misrepresentation.**
5.   **He Listened To Those Not Able To Explain Themselves Thoroughly And Adequately.**

Solomon Knew Listening Would Reveal The Cause And Cure of Any Strife Around Him. "Cast out the scorner, and contention shall go out; yea, strife and reproach shall cease," he says in Proverbs 22:10.

7 Facts You Should Know About Conflict

1.   **Conflict Occurs.**
2.   **Your Reaction To Conflict Determines Whether It Is A Barricade or A Bridge To Your Future.** You must face it.
3.   **You Cannot Correct What You Are Unwilling To Confront.**
4.   **Conflict Is Always Caused By Wrong Words.**
5.   **Never Attempt To Change Someone Who Is Unwilling To Change.**
6.   **Wrong People Create Wrong Climates.**
7.   **Conflict Always Has A Cure.** The cure is to remove the person who insists on speaking those wrong words. Proverbs 26:20-22 says, "Where no wood is

there the fire goeth out: so where there is no talebearer, the strife ceaseth. As coals are to burning coals, and wood to fire; so is a contentious man to kindle strife. The words of a talebearer are as wounds, and they go down into the innermost parts of the belly."

Solomon was a trained listener. He always listened to both sides before making a decision. This is one of the Golden Secrets that helped him become The Richest Man Who Ever Lived.

Business Is Simply Solving A Problem For An Agreed Reward.

-MIKE MURDOCK

≈ 14 ≈

SOLOMON INSISTED ON DETAILED CONTRACTS

Always Read The Fine Print.

A few nights ago, I saw an advertisement for exercise equipment on television. As I watched, I grew more and more excited. The merchandise was being offered for a very reasonable price. Then I looked the second time.

The price splashed across the screen was not really the price of the equipment; it was the amount of each *monthly* installment. At first I was disappointed. Then, I realized that almost every transaction in business is just like this. It is so important to read every detail of a contract and make certain you understand it clearly.

Solomon, The Richest Man Who Ever Lived, understood the importance of covenant and making a precise and well-understood agreement. We read in 1 Kings 5:12 that he and Hiram, the king of Tyre, "made a league together."

5 Facts And Keys To Solomon's Success With Contracts

1. **Solomon Was Detailed In His Expectations.** "Now therefore command thou that they hew me cedar trees out of Lebanon," he says in 1 Kings 5:6.

2. **Solomon Was Detailed In Who He Would Hire.** "Unto thee will I give hire for thy servants according to all that thou shalt appoint," he says in 1 Kings 5:6.

3. **Solomon Defined In Detail What Kind of Compensation Others Could Expect.** First Kings 5:11 says, "And Solomon gave Hiram twenty thousand measures of wheat for food to his household, and twenty measures of pure oil."

4. **Solomon Was Detailed About The Payment Schedule.** "Thus gave Solomon to Hiram year by year," he says in 1 Kings 5:11.

5. **Solomon's Contracts Were Always A Win-Win Situation For All Parties Involved.** Hiram was also pleased by the contract. In 1 Kings 5:9, he says, "And thou shalt accomplish my desire, in giving food for my household."

Ronald Reagan, the former president known as the "Great Communicator," irritated foreign dignitaries with his statement, "Trust, but verify." Nevertheless, this policy protected the United States repeatedly.

Youth *trust*.

The wise *test*.

"You can trust me" is a common statement in many circles. Solomon and experienced men like him know better. Words can be misinterpreted, forgotten or conveniently ignored.

Contracts have an important place in our world today.

4 Warnings To Remember Before Signing A Contract

1. **Always** **Hire** **An** **Independent,**

Competent Lawyer To Analyze The Details of Every Contract. Having a professional on your side is vital. He or she can often anticipate a problem that you could not possibly imagine.

One of the finest lawyers I have ever known, Dennis Brewer, was reviewing a contract with me one day. Though I had examined that contract from every conceivable angle, he saw a potential problem that had never even crossed my mind. His many years of experience reminded him of a situation that had come up. He helped me avoid a possible trap that could have resulted in great pain.

Robert S. McNamara is considered by many to have been one of the most brilliant men ever in government. At one time, he was the vice president in charge of the Ford Division and later would become the Secretary of Defense under the Kennedy administration.

On page 42 of his book, *Straight Talk,* Lee Iacocca wrote, "McNamara was also one of the smartest men I've ever met, with a phenomenal IQ and a steel-trap mind. He was a mental giant. With his amazing capacity to absorb facts, he also retained everything he learned. But McNamara would more than want your facts—he also knew the hypothetical ones. When you talked with him, you realized that he'd already played out of his head the relevant details for every conceivable option and scenario. He taught me never to make a major decision without having a choice of at least vanilla or chocolate. And if more than $100 million was at stake, it was a good idea to have strawberry too."

2.   Consider   Every   Conceivable

Consequence of A Contract. Two years ago, I sat down in a Christian television studio to share some songs and participate in a telethon. I was brought a contract to sign and it seemed a little strange to me. The contract stated that they would have the right to re-air and play anything I said or did the entire evening anytime, anywhere and under any circumstance. I refused. I will never sign a contract giving someone unlimited right to use my statements supporting someone I have never met. Details matter greatly.

3. **Never Agree To Anything That Someone Is Unwilling To Write Down In A Contract.** You see, the force of a personality or the atmosphere created to "romance" you can often deceive you into ignoring the true facts. I have been talked into things I later regretted. Then I remembered that I was being pressured by someone's aggressiveness and even influenced by their "weapon of hospitality."

4. **Beware of The Weapon of Hospitality.** Recently, I read a fascinating story by a successful American businessman. He flew overseas to complete a business transaction and was to remain there for five days. When he arrived, he was whisked into a whirlwind tour of the country. He hardly slept. He kept asking to see the contracts, which were the reason he had taken the trip in the first place. They murmured that first they wanted to show their hospitality.

Days later, moments before he was to leave for the airport, the contracts were brought out. He stated that his mind was so distracted and fragmented, his body so weary, he hardly knew what he was doing. That's when he realized their entire scheme was to break his focus, wear him down, and force him to make a last-minute decision. When he refused, they were indignant and angry. He insisted on bringing the contracts back to the states where they would be carefully reviewed.

Robert McNamara, the legendary vice president of Ford Division, taught Lee Iacocca to *write down* everything in *detail*—away from the torrent of words and the influence of a persuasive personality. "Go home tonight and put your great idea on paper. If you can't do that, then you haven't really thought it out."

Lee Iacocca commented, "It was a valuable lesson, and I've followed his lead ever since. Whenever one of my people has an idea, I ask him to lay it out in writing. I don't want anyone to sell me on a plan just by the melodiousness of his voice or force of his personality. You really can't afford that."

In his book, *Straight Talk,* he continues, "As I'd learned from McNamara, *the discipline of writing something down is the first step toward making it happen.* In conversation, you can get away with all kinds of vagueness and nonsense, often without even realizing it. But there's something about putting your thoughts on paper that forces you to get down to specifics. It's harder to deceive yourself—or anybody else."

Always insist on written and detailed contracts on matters of great importance. This is one of the Golden Secrets that helped Solomon become The Richest Man Who Ever Lived.

The Mystery
of Excellence Is
Always Locked
In The Seed of Time.

-MIKE MURDOCK

≈ 15 ≈

SOLOMON ALWAYS HIRED THE BEST OF THE BEST

Excellence Requires Pursuit.

Quality is not commonplace. It is not always accessible. It is not always convenient. It is rarely inexpensive. Excellence will cost you. But, the rewards of excellence are lasting.

Solomon wanted the highest quality craftsmen in brass. He sent for Hiram. In 1 Kings 7:14, Hiram is described as a man, "filled with Wisdom, and understanding, and cunning to work all works in brass."

Solomon wanted the most skilled sailors in his navy. When Solomon created his navy, he says in 1 Kings 9:27, that he chose, "shipmen that had knowledge of the sea."

Solomon loved beautiful woodwork and insisted on hiring only the best craftsmen. First Kings 5:6 says, "For thou knowest that there is not among us any that can skill to hew timber like unto the Sidonians."

In his great book, *Salesman of the Century,* Ron Popeil, one of the multimillionaires you see on television so often wrote, "I realized a long time ago that I'm not an expert in every area. That's why I work with professionals to assist me in the creation and marketing of my products. I do know what consumers like and how to market a product, but I know very little about engineering, about motors and how things work internally. *So I bring in professionals* to work with me and have always been fortunate to surround myself with people who I always felt were a lot smarter."

7 Facts About Excellence

1. Excellence Is Always Instantly Recognized. Uncommon men honor it in friends and foes alike. As Porter Bibb, the biographer of famed multimillionaire Ted Turner, wrote on page 65 of his book, *It Ain't As Easy As It Looks,* "He is quick to compliment worthy opponents."

2. Excellence Never Produces Regret And Remorse. Someone said, "The quality of your product will be remembered long after the price of it has been forgotten." Whether you are hiring an employee or purchasing an item at your local store, when you invest in the best, it creates peace of mind that is unexplainable. You have just improved the quality of your life, and your inner peace is the proof.

3. Excellence Never Requires Replacement. Have you ever used an inferior product in order to save a few dollars? Of course you have. And within a matter of a few months, it had to be replaced.

4. Excellence Enables You To Focus. Solomon knew the importance of focus. Anything less than the best becomes distracting. Something *within* you is always in pursuit of the best. The desire for excellence is a natural current running within every human heart. It is unexplainable, undeniable and always emerging.

5. Any Refusal To Invest In Excellence Guarantees A Future Loss. I had a disheartening experience some years ago. When a contract was presented to me, I decided to save the $200 cost of taking it to my lawyer. Twelve months later, one word in the contract cost me $10,000. Think about it! What a terrible trade-off! In my desire to save $200, I lost $10,000—simply because I refused to hire the best, the most qualified, the specialist in the center of his expertise.

"Why are you doing your own tax return?" I inquired of a close friend.

"I'm saving $120," was his reply.

How foolish! Before me was a young man who knew nothing about taxes, tax laws or the dangers of making a mistake. You see, there are some who spend thousands of hours reviewing, analyzing and scrutinizing the latest laws and the most recent tax breaks, in order to help us avoid pitfalls that cost us thousands of dollars. It is foolish to ignore their expertise, their gifts and skills.

One of the most successful men on television today is Ron Popeil. When he advises people about setting up their new home shopping business, he knows what he is talking about. On page 243 of his book, *The Salesman of the Century,* he says, "In setting up your new home shopping business, you're probably thinking that you can sit at home, answer the phone, ship the parts out yourself and become an instant millionaire. Wrong. *Let the professionals do what they do."*

6. Excellence Permits The Qualified To Perform. Arrogance will not reach for others, but humility recognizes that others possess something you do not. Solomon showed humility by honoring the skills in others. He was a long-term thinker. *He refused to* *carry any burden another was qualified to shoulder.*

7. Selecting Persons of Excellence To Surround You Is The Most Important Skill A Leader Can Develop. Hiring the right people to help you nurture and achieve your dream is the most important thing you will ever undertake. "That's an important skill to have, because the most important thing a manager can do is hire the right new people," says Lee Iacocca, the legendary automobile mogul, on page 23 of his revealing book, *Straight Talk.*

The famed real estate tycoon, Donald Trump, wrote, "My philosophy is always to hire the best from the best," explaining one of his Master Keys of Success. He goes to the best companies in search of their best employees. Then he looks for ways to get them to come to work for him.

Some hire the *available.*

Some hire the *least expensive.*

Some hire the least *intimidating.*

Some hire the least *demanding.*

Some hire the *likable.*

And, some hire their *relatives!*

Why do many ignore the skills of specialists and experts? Why do they attempt to do everything themselves?

People Do Not Insist On The Best For The Following 3 Reasons

1. Experts Are Usually More *Expensive.*

2. Experts Are Not Always *Accessible* When You Need Them.

3. Experts Require Pursuit, *Patience* And Persistence.

The Richest Man Who Ever Lived Knew What He Was Doing. Hiring the best of the best liberated him to focus on his own expertise. It freed him and it guaranteed the longevity of his dream, the admiration of other quality people and peace of mind.

Solomon always hired the best of the best. This is one of the Golden Secrets that helped him to become The Richest Man Who Ever Lived.

Hurrying Is The Weakness of Passion.

-MIKE MURDOCK

≈ 16 ≈

SOLOMON REFUSED TO HURRY

Great Dreams Require Time.

Solomon's incredible feat, the building of God's holy Temple, was not accomplished in twelve weeks or six months or even a year. Solomon invested seven long and fruitful years to complete it. We read in 1 Kings 6:38, "So was he seven years in building it."

He was not in a hurry.

Solomon took the time necessary to develop essential relationships with kings, skilled craftsmen and thousands of workers.

Dexter Yager has helped thousands escape the claws of poverty. He understands the power of time and using the "Weapon of Waiting." I urge you to read his unforgettable book, *A Millionaire's Common Sense Approach To Wealth.*

On pages 95 and 96, he writes, "I sometimes buy properties that I will keep for ten, fifteen, twenty years. Sometimes I keep them longer than that in order to make them as profitable as possible. My pattern is to go into an area, eye property, see something potentially valuable, buy it at a low price because it's yet undeveloped, and hold on to it long enough to see the investment grow in value. Being a long ranger, I often make many, many times my initial investment."

Dexter also notes that Donald Trump refused to hurry on some important investments, "Donald Trump said recently that the reason he was able to make great money out of some of his properties was because he had *staying* power. He has enough money to stick with it when others cannot hold out."

Anything Significant In Your Life Will Require Uncommon Time. When you hurry, you destroy the very thing you are wanting to create.

9 Helpful Hints For Those Who Tend To Hurry

1.   When You Hurry, You Increase The Mistakes You Make. Sometimes, those mistakes can be almost fatal. At the very least, you have succeeded only in slowing your project down.

2.   When You Hurry, You Often Have To Redo Everything You Have Done. Mechanics who hurry often see their customer return the second time because something was left unfinished. They receive a midnight call from the person whose automobile is broken down on the side of the road—all because they hurried. This increases the expense of the repair to the mechanic.

3.   When You Slow Down, You Follow The Example of Other Uncommon Achievers. Multi-millionaire Ron Popeil writes on page 195 of his excellent book, *Salesman of the Century,* "The key to the whole plan is sometimes taking things one step at a time. Be very methodical. Don't be in too much of a rush."

4.   Slowing Down Provides Time To Receive

Worthy Counsel. On page 467 of his wonderful book, *An American Journey,* Colin Powell wrote the following regarding President George Bush, "He had listened quietly to his advisors. He had consulted by phone with royal leaders. And then, taking his own counsel, he had come to this momentous decision and revealed it at the first opportunity."

5. One Moment of Hurry Can Create One Month of Chaos. It happened to me a few days ago. I rushed out of a room too quickly and left an expensive cellular phone plugged into the wall. Fortunately, it was returned about ten days later. Meanwhile, I had to do without my phone. Guard against hurrying, especially while traveling.

6. Permitting Others To Hurry You On An Important Project Will Only Hurt You. I learned this lesson during the production of one of my most exciting books. I looked it over, but I really did not want to lose a week by using a proofreader. What should have been a joy became a constant source of irritation as people across the country wrote to tell me about typographical errors.

Another book I wrote was edited by a publisher. The editor added sentences to an illustration that were totally incorrect. But when they sent me the manuscript for approval, I was rushing out the door. I glanced quickly through the book and said, "It looks good to me." Later as I carefully read the book, I was shocked to see these incorrect statements.

7. Refusing To Hurry Removes The Potential Burden of Buyer's Remorse. Avoid the temptation to hurry when making major purchases. Several years ago, I rushed into a decision about purchasing a car for my mother. I was excited. As I stood there looking the car over, something inside spoke to me, "Wait. Do not buy this car right now. Do not rush it." I ignored that inner voice and purchased it. It turned out to be one of the worse purchases of my life. She never really liked the color and the car broke down constantly. These are the results you can expect when *hurrying*.

Look back at the biggest mistakes you have made in your life. You were in a hurry, weren't you!

8. Allowing Others To Hurry You Into Marriage Can Create A Lifetime of Heartache. One of my dear friends became lonely and anxious to "get my wife and settle down." He ignored my counsel to invest time in developing the relationship. (You see, it takes time for wonderful qualities to appear. It often takes time for weaknesses and frailties to appear as well.) He hurried his marriage and it became a source of great heartache to him.

9. Investing Time In Seasons of Personal Restoration Is One of The Wisest Decisions You Can Make. Jesus, Himself, took time away from the crowds to recuperate and restore Himself. He instructed His disciples, "Come ye apart and rest a while," (Mark 6:31). This observation in the ancient writings is one of the most important laws of life.

> ▶ Are you pursuing a relationship? Give it *time*.
>
> ▶ Are you building a great business? Invest time in careful planning.
>
> ▶ Do you want a dream home? You won't be sorry if you take time to collect information from a variety of vendors and gather a

number of estimates.

▶ *Do not rush life.* It was meant to be *tasted,* not swallowed.

Solomon knew this and developed and collected the greatest amount of wealth known to mankind.

The legendary billionaire, Sam Walton, said, "I never invest in a company for where it will be in eighteen months. I always look at where it will be in ten years." He never hurried; he was a long-term thinker.

The reasons men hurry are varied. Some want to get a product on the market before their competition. Sometimes, items are offered at an incredible bargain or so it may seem if we are in a hurry. Sometimes, it is good to get a product on the market during an appropriate season such as Christmas. All of these reasons for moving quickly are valid and wonderful.

The difference is in the quality.

I am not recommending *a passive attitude.*

Please understand me. I believe that aggressiveness is an admirable trait. Diligence is always rewarded. Sluggishness is not a quality of a successful man. I am not talking about "taking your own good time." I am not encouraging you to stop everything you are doing until the world around you comes to a crawl.

Do Things Right The First Time.

Solomon took the time necessary to produce a dream at its highest possible level of excellence. He believed it is always better to do one thing right than three things half right.

Solomon even refused to hurry his conversations with others. "Seest thou a man that is hasty in his words? there is more hope of a fool than of him," he says in Proverbs 29:20.

Refusing to hurry is one of the wisest qualities of
the Uncommon Achiever. It is one of the Golden Secrets
that helped Solomon become The Richest Man Who
Ever Lived.

≈ 17 ≈

SOLOMON WILLINGLY SOWED THE MIRACLE SEED OF TIME TOWARD HIS DREAM

Time Consciousness Is The Greatest Difference Between The Poor And The Prosperous.

As I have mentioned several times, the famed billionaire Sam Walton refused to invest in a company based on what it would become in eighteen months or two years. He was a long-term thinker. He studied what the company would become within ten years. He thought *generationally.*

Recently, someone explained that the average American business is based on a five-year plan. The most successful and effective Japanese companies create 100-year plans. The difference is profound.

Time is truly the greatest and most significant gift you have ever received on earth.

Think about it.

Time Is The Currency of Earth.

You have traded time for everything you have. You have been unwilling to trade time for everything you do not have.

"I really wish I could lose ten pounds," lamented a

friend recently. "But, I simply do not have the time to go to a health spa and work out every day. I just wish I had the time to do it!" Now that very evening my friend watched a television movie for two hours. She was willing to exchange her time for entertainment, but not for a healthy body. *Whatever You Do Not Possess Right Now, You Have Been Unwilling To Sow The Seed of Time To Produce.*

A major difference exists between the poor and the powerful; the pauper and the prosperous. That difference is *the management of Time.* Consider what I wrote earlier:

> ▶ *I have never met an impoverished person who was conscious of Time.*
> ▶ *I have never met a prosperous person who was not conscious of Time.*

I would never hire anyone who refuses to wear a watch or have an answering machine on their telephone. Why? Because their indifferent attitude toward Time is a prediction of their life. Time is the most precious gift we are given in this life. When we are unwilling to protect, cherish and celebrate it, we have deliberately sabotaged the master key to successful living.

I shared this recently at a conference. When I finished, a young man came up to me and laughingly said, "When I want to know the time, I simply ask everyone around me. They tell me!"

He missed my point and in a few short sentences had managed to reveal a major flaw in his character. It was tragic to hear that he deliberately squanders the gift of Time he has been given. It was even more tragic to see his willingness to destroy the focus and gift of

Time for those around him.

The greatest concert pianists on earth invested their most precious gift to develop their talent—the gift of *Time*.

The greatest painters our world has known, those whose work adorns our museums today, invested their greatest gift in the development of their talent—the gift of *Time*.

Show me the barren forest of friendships where the leaves have been stripped, and I will show you a forest where the Seed of Time has not been sown.

Show me the empty desert of dreams where creativity has never flourished, and I will show you a desert where the Seed of Time has not been sown.

The gift of Time is also evident on the other side of extraordinary and uncommon achievements. When you open a health magazine to see a sculptured, firm and healthy body, you see that the Seed of Time has been sown.

Show me *greatness*, and I will show you someone who has purchased success with the currency called "Time."

Show me an uncommon, flourishing and prosperous business, and I will show you someone who has planted the Seed of Time deep in the soil.

Picture a lovely, relaxing afternoon drive in the countryside. As you slow to turn a corner, you look to your right and imagine this scene: bushes, weeds and thick brush, a sagging barbed-wire fence, leaves piled so deep that you can barely see through the brush, thorn bushes growing high and wild. Running is impossible, and a walk would quickly become a cutting, flesh-tearing, difficult experience with limbs tearing at your shoulders and thorns and thistles ripping your face. In your wildest imagination, can you imagine anyone investing their money in that thick foliage and wild branches of this forest?

It is a most undesirable place. In fact, your instinct is to speed up to leave this distasteful scene behind as quickly as possible.

Now imagine that you drive a few miles down the road. As you come up over a big hill, heading for the freeway, you suddenly look off to the right again. The scene is breathtaking. Beautiful trees line a winding road with a gate. Flowers of every color dot the landscape. The grass is cut neatly and close to the ground. It looks like twenty full-time gardeners have sculptured the landscape just for you. It seems like Heaven on earth. You drive through the lovely park-like atmosphere and see your friends waiting inside the open gate.

What made the difference? *Someone took the Seed of Time and turned a jungle into a park.* Pulling weeds, pruning bushes and trees, and carefully sowing Time have created a small paradise.

Every time you drive down the highway, you can see where the Seeds of Time have been sown. The ugly places never received such attention. The beautiful places were costly, but the rewards are limitless.

Now, picture your life's journey. As you pass through the jungle moments of your life where the bristles, thorns and brush make passage impossible, remember that the Seed of Time can make the jungle a paradise. It may be a relationship or a struggling business that could not get off the ground.

The Seed of Time is the Unrecognized Ingredient.

Show me the Uncommon Child—confident, enthusiastic and zealous for his or her dreams and goals. Somebody has sowed the Seed called "Time."

Show me the laughter, exuberance and vibrant excitement of a teenager going to work each afternoon, and I will show you a life where the Seed of Time has been sown.

Solomon understood that the hidden secret of excellence is the investment of time, whether the goal is to become physically fit, build a beautiful home, or establish a thriving business.

The Mystery of Excellence is always locked in the Seed called "Time."

Solomon had a dream. He felt that it was his destiny to build a holy Temple that would honor the God of the universe. He had thousands of employees at his call and the resources to pay any amount of money he saw fit. Many countries desired to participate in his project.

But he was not hurried.

He did not rush.

He understood the mysterious, miraculous power of the tiny Seed that grows the "Garden of Greatness"— the Seed called "Time."

The poor often get hurried. Some want to get rich quick—overnight. Many will stand in line for nearly an hour waiting to buy a lottery ticket, but few will sit for two hours each week in a local college classroom waiting to receive the Wisdom and understanding they need. Some spend more money on lottery tickets than they invest in books each month. They do not understand the miracle Seed called Time.

Some parents throw money at their problem

children. They will purchase the nicest cars, send them on the longest vacations, and buy the name-brand clothes that bring approval from their peers. But when they refuse to sow the miracle Seed called "Time," they often lose everything.

Where do you spend most of your Time each week? Your answer will reveal what you love the *most*.

Uncommon Friendships require uncommon Time.

Uncommon Marriages require uncommon Time.

Uncommon Businesses require uncommon Time.

Now, here are some important questions you must ask yourself. How much Time are you willing to *invest* in order to build a great dream for your future? How much Time are you willing to invest to research and *gather information* about your dream? How much Time are you willing to invest in planning *each day* of your life? How much Time are you willing to spend to develop an *understanding* of those around you?

It takes more Time to build a skyscraper than to build a small log cabin. Far more time is required to build a Rolls Royce than to build a bicycle.

Is your dream really important to you? Is it important enough to absorb your time and attention? If you aren't persuaded that it is worthy of your Time, you will never empty your life into it.

Solomon took seven years to build the Temple— seven long and difficult years. Seven years of negotiating contracts. But in 1 Kings 6:38, we see that his dream was big enough to sow the Seed of Time into it.

▶ Find something *bigger* than yourself.

▶ Find something worth depositing *your whole life* into.

► Find something that will take several *years* to *achieve.*

Then rally every ounce of energy behind it. Link every relationship and friendship into it.

Time is the secret of the wealthy.

The wealthy think generationally. They think long-term. Very few poor people leave any legacy for their children. Their obsession is survival, not succession. It is the mystery of success—the ability to think *beyond* your present.

Your Energy Will Only Last As Long As Your Focus. So focus on a long-term goal. This generates energy, enthusiasm and the life to sustain you for the present.

11 Power Keys That Will Help You Use Your Time Wisely

1. **Invest Whatever Time Is Necessary To Produce The Highest Level of Excellence Possible In Your Work.** My graphics artist is a rare young man who lives in North Carolina. His work surpasses that of anyone I have ever known. He is meticulous in every detail. I recently contacted him concerning an urgent project.

"Chris, I desperately need the cover of a new book. But I am going to press immediately and I need your attention. Can you possibly work on it tonight and finish it in the next two days?"

"Dr. Murdock, you know me. I will do my best to accommodate your schedule," he replied. However, I will not permit anything to go out with my name on it that is not the best I can possibly make it. I will not do sloppy work or any cover that I would be ashamed of. Give it to someone else if you have to, or *give me the time I need to do the best job."*

That's the secret of his extraordinary gift.

Martin Luther King, Jr. said it well. "If a man is called to be a street sweeper, he should sweep streets even as Michael Angelo painted, or Beethoven composed music or Shakespeare wrote poetry. He should sweep streets so well that all the host of Heaven and earth will pause to say, 'Here lived a great street sweeper who did his job well.'"

Someone has said, "The quality of your product will be remembered long after the price you charged for it is forgotten."

Do not start anything you do not intend to finish *well*.

2. Put Quality Into Every Conversation In Which You Are A Part. When you open your mouth, speak clearly, appropriately and completely. Strive for excellence in every word that leaves your mouth. Put Thought into it. Put Time into it. Build the consciousness of quality in every single situation of your life.

3. Guard The Access You Permit Others. Everyone should not have the same freedom toward your life. Intimacy should be *earned*. I refuse to allow anybody to walk off the streets and "meet me for an appointment."

My goals are *golden*.

My plans are *prosperous*.

My appointments must be *appropriate*.

Booker T. Washington once said, "Excellence is to do a common thing in an uncommon way."

Qualify anyone who enters your personal arena of life. What is the criteria for relationship?

> ▶ That person must truly *desire* something you possess and *be willing to pay the price* for

receiving it.

▶ That person must possess something you desire from them and be willing to impart it to you.

4. Recognize Your Personal "Seeds Of Time" As Golden Coins You Place In The Hands of Another. If you saw a child throw a $500 gold piece into the gutter, would you hand him several more gold coins? Only a fool would do that. Yet every day, grubby, greedy, and clutching hands grab the gold coins of your Time and throw them into the wind. Guard against this by *pinpointing parasite relationships.* Avoid problem people who do not value the gold coins called Time.

5. Invest Time With The Mentors Who Impart To You. Your mentor has something you cannot receive from anyone else on earth. To receive it, you must linger long enough in his presence for the impartation to emerge.

6. Take Time To Establish A Reputation For Integrity. Solomon knew that, "A good name is rather to be chosen than great riches." You can read this instruction in Proverbs 22:1.

7. Control The Climate And Time of Every Appointment. I mentioned this earlier. It's worthy of emphasis. When someone schedules to meet you at 3:00, schedule the end of your appointment at the same time. "I will meet you from 3:00 to 3:30." Why is this so important? If a person comes twenty minutes late to the appointment, he or she has decided the briefness of your moments together. You now have only ten minutes left. You see, *everything you do educates those around you.* When you allow your time to be treated lightly, time with you becomes less meaningful.

8.   Begin Training Those Around You To Respect Your Time.   Do not become obnoxious or overbearing about it. Stay kind, but firm.

Recently, a young man wanted to meet with me. Though my schedule was full and my projects were behind, he seemed so insistent I decided to reschedule all of my projects to accommodate him. At the last moment, he phoned.

"I'm involved in a project, and I really cannot get away for this appointment," he explained. He wanted to know if we could meet at another time. I explained that I too had many projects. I told him I understood and that if I ever felt that it could occur, I would call him and let him know.

Few People Around You Have Any Serious Plans They Are Pursuing On A Daily Basis.   Their lunches can run two hours, and they never think twice. They lack focus and purpose. These kinds of friends will sabotage the golden dreams in your lifetime.

9.   Your Dream Will Require Much More Time Than You Realize.

▶ *You Will Require Time For Preparation.*   The time you spend in college, at special seminars and training, will prepare you for your dream. It is well worth the investment.

▶ *You Will Require Time For Negotiation.*   You will have to negotiate costs, the salaries of those who assist you, the purchase of a new building for your business. Take time to understand the importance of negotiation.

10. An Uncommon Dream Will Require Uncommon Meditation.   Think on it. Meditate on it. Study your dreams and goals from every conceivable perspective. What you keep looking at, you will eventually see. What you look at the longest, becomes the strongest in your mind.

Solomon knew this secret. In Ecclesiastes 3:1-3, he wrote, "To every thing there is a season, and a time to every purpose under the Heaven: A time to be born, and a time to die; a time to plant, and a time to pluck up that which is planted; A time to kill, and a time to heal; a time to break down, and a time to build up."

Solomon fully recognized the inevitable and irreplaceable rewards of patience. It took seven long, difficult, and painful years to build the Temple. But, he achieved his dream. In Galatians 6:9, we read, "And let us not be weary in well doing: for in due season we shall reap, if we faint not."

11. Invest In A Time-Management Plan Book.

▶ Make it *small enough* to carry with you and keep it handy at all times.

▶ It should be *big enough* for you to write down your dreams and goals for each day and week.

▶ Explore various types of day-timers.

▶ Question those around you who are leading productive lives. Ask them their advice concerning the creation of a time-management notebook.

▶ Make the extra effort to discipline your life for *thirty days.*

▶ Write out a clear-cut plan each day and work to develop a conscious *awareness* of time.

Solomon used the "Seed of Time" to grow the greatest achievement of his lifetime. It is one of the Golden Secrets that helped him become The Richest Man Who Ever Lived.

Your Self-Portrait
Determines The Kind
of Enemy You Are
Willing To Confront.

-MIKE MURDOCK

⋙ 18 ⋘

SOLOMON WILLINGLY CONFRONTED HIS ADVERSARIES

Conflict Is Sometimes Unavoidable.

Solomon recognized that peace often follows war. Battle is sometimes necessary for peace. In fact, Solomon, whose name means "peaceful," enjoyed a peaceful reign of forty years.

Some might think it strange that Solomon was the first king to establish a navy. He produced more people capable of going to war than anyone before him. *That was one of his keys to keeping peace.* As the beloved former president, Ronald Reagan, often stressed, Solomon believed in "peace through *strength*."

Troublemakers always emerge. When they do, confrontation is often necessary to remove them.

David, Solomon's father, was one of the most famed and effective soldiers who ever lived. He killed a bear and lion bare-handed as a shepherd boy, and he understood planning, attack and ambush. King David knew how to get into the mind of his enemy and make the decisions that would cause that enemy to fall. He could adapt behavior that created confusion or generated energy. The same David who danced with fervent passion before the Lord and his people, infusing them with energy, also babbled like a fool, spit dripping from his mouth, to create the idea that he was insane and fool the enemy.

Obviously David mentored Solomon thoroughly in warfare. In 1 Kings 2, we read, that he counseled him concerning his personal enemies and advised him regarding his friends and those qualified to sit at his table. But he also gave Solomon his full approval to aggressively pursue the complete destruction of his enemies.

Solomon did so. His half brother, Adonijah, requested through Bathsheba, Abishag the Shunammite woman, be given to him to be his wife, Solomon's anger erupted. We read in 1 Kings 2:20 that Abishag was a beautiful, young virgin. She had served as a companion for David in the closing years of his life. Yet, Adonijah had such disrespect for spiritual protocol that he wanted to take this woman to his own bed. (See 1 Kings 2:23-25.) Solomon had him killed immediately.

Why? Tolerance would have sent the wrong message. Solomon remembered well the compromises of his father, David. Because his father had not dealt strongly with Absalom and others, the kingdom was stolen from him.

Enemies are costly—too costly to avoid confrontation.

Yes, Solomon loved peace and sought after peace. But he was also a passionate man concerning right and wrong. He was the son of two adulterers, and the first husband of his mother had been murdered by his own father. He understood the cost of war. But he also understood the devastating cost of compromise.

Solomon knew the rewards of persistence, tenacity

and confrontation. He understood that compromise can bring about tragic consequences. He stood firm in his determination to recognize his adversaries and confront them.

Today the rules of civilization are obviously different. With the exception of war, we negotiate with enemies rather than killing them. We confront them through contracts, laws and principles.

7 Important Facts You Should Remember When Confronting Your Enemies Effectively

1. **An Enemy Will Expose Your Weaknesses.** This is important. Until you understand your weaknesses, you can never unleash your strengths. On page 32 of his excellent book, *A Millionaire's Notebook,* Steven K. Scott, co-founder of the American Telecast Corporation encourages readers to, "List what you consider your greatest weaknesses, both personally and professionally—lack of education, lack of career achievement, patience, short tempered, etc."

You see, you cannot correct your weaknesses until you recognize them. You cannot appreciate those who can help you achieve your goals and dreams until you first understand where you need help.

2. **An Enemy Forces You To Determine The Worthiness of Your Goals And Dreams.** Without an enemy, you may waste your time pursuing something that doesn't matter at all.

3. **Enemies Should Be Confronted Quickly.** A former governor of New Hampshire and chief of staff for a former president made an interesting observation.

He said that he managed by the "Acorn Philosophy." He dealt with the problem when it was the size of an acorn instead of waiting until it became the size of an oak tree. Such a philosophy helps to stop problems before they affect everyone else.

    4.   An Enemy Often Uses Someone You Love.

    5.   An Enemy Often Uses Someone You Trust.

    6.   An Enemy Often Uses The Most Vulnerable People Around You.

    7.   Different Enemies Use Different Methods To Deceive You.

Solomon sat at the feet of a warrior father, a man who knew the cost of bringing home the spoils. He was not afraid of war. He was aware of the importance of confronting his enemies. The "payoff" was worth it.

Confronting your adversaries is one of the Golden Secrets that helped Solomon become The Richest Man Who Ever Lived.

∾ 19 ∾

SOLOMON KEPT ALIVE THE ENTHUSIASM AND GREATNESS OF HIS DREAM

Anything Can Die, Even A Dream.

Anything neglected will deteriorate. It could be a vibrant marriage or the dream of your life.

Solomon understood the importance of *motivating* others. He continuously stayed in contact with builders, employees and those involved with his dream. He knew that *their enthusiasm* depended upon *his energy.* Their focus was kept alive and defined through his constant communication.

Ancient writings record his constant courtship of those necessary for the fulfillment and completion of his dream.

He kept reminding the people of the *greatness* of his dream. In 1 Kings 8:17-20, we read, "And it was in the heart of David my father to build an house for the name of the Lord God of Israel. And the Lord said unto David my father, Whereas it was in thine heart to build an house unto My Name, thou didst well that it was in thine heart. Nevertheless thou shalt not build the house; but thy son that shall come forth out of thy loins, he shall build the house unto My Name. And the Lord hath performed His Word that He spake, and I am risen up in the room of David my father, and sit on the throne of Israel, as the Lord promised, and have built an house for the name of the Lord God of Israel."

One of the wealthiest men in America, Donald Trump, wrote, "The minute I get back to my office, I *start returning calls.*"

I once read where one multimillionaire calls his office at least *ten times every day.*

You see, those around you are plagued with constant interruptions and distractions. They need your energy, encouragement and protection of their *focus.*

What is the biggest dream in your heart today? What do you long to *finish?* What would you attempt to do if you knew it was impossible for you to fail?

4 Power Keys That Will Unleash The Force of Enthusiasm Around You

1. **Create A Beautiful Visual Photograph of Your Dream And Place It On The Wall That You Look At Every Day.** Feast on it. Discuss it. Talk about it. Think about it. You must keep your vision before you.

2. **Take A Tiny Step Every Day Toward Your Big Dream.** Sometimes, small steps create big joys within you. The smallest step in the right direction always generates joy. Take enough small steps and you will find increasing energy and desire to accomplish your dream.

3. **Assemble A Support Team That Believes**

In Your Dream. They will encourage you and be your cheerleaders. Carefully choose the people you want to be close to you.

4.   **Realize That You Are Responsible For Maintaining Your Own Enthusiasm And Energy For Achieving The Dream of Your Life.** It is not the responsibility of your husband or wife. It is *your* dream and *your* life. You must take the steps necessary to create a climate of continuous victory concerning your dream!

Solomon understood this. He celebrated everything, including the power of ceremony and atmosphere. *Keeping his dream alive* is one of the Golden Secrets that helped him become The Richest Man Who Ever Lived.

When Wrong People
Leave Your Life
Wrong Things
Stop Happening.

-MIKE MURDOCK

≈ 20 ≈

SOLOMON REFUSED TO TOLERATE EVEN THE SLIGHTEST DISLOYALTY

Disloyalty Is Cancerous And Deadly.

Disloyalty is an invisible, silent and often unnoticed decision by someone close to you to destroy your dream and participate in your downfall. This individual is the worst kind of enemy you will ever have in your life.

Counterspies almost always receive life sentences. Why? Because courts do not deal lightly with someone who is a silent, invisible destroyer of the nation in which they live. A spy from another country will get off with a lighter sentence than a citizen whose disloyalty has caused the death of many.

Treason is not merely a character *flaw*. It is the *absence* of character—a purposeful decision to use the information they have to destroy their own nation.

Solomon had watched his father, King David, make the mistake of his lifetime—*the tolerance of disloyalty*. I would encourage you to read this unforgettable story from 1 Kings 2. Solomon watched the tragedy unfold before his eyes on a daily basis.

Absalom was the handsome son of David. He envied the splendor, popularity and prosperity of his father. So he would stand and greet the people personally outside the palace each day. Like tiny *drops of poison,* his words fell into the ears of the citizens of Israel. He sowed uncertainty, doubt and discord by insinuating that David was too busy to really listen to their concerns or care about their difficulties and tears. He made himself available to them and literally stole the hearts of the people David had led for so many years. One of the most vile acts became his habit—he slept with his father's concubines.

Absalom did not have a character *flaw.*

Absalom had no character.

He flaunted his sin. He sneered at the greatness of his father. And yet David did not confront him properly. As David permitted him to continue to live and exist, Solomon watched this charade parade before him. He saw the kingdom come apart because of David's tolerance of wrong people close to him. When General Joab defied David's instructions by killing Absalom, disrespect for David was obvious.

In some ways, Solomon was wiser than his father, David. He reigned in peace for many years, primarily because he dealt swiftly and decisively with disloyalty. David permitted disloyalty to linger and his entire reign was one of warfare.

The story recorded in 1 Kings 2 is quite detailed. Solomon's brother Adonijah desired the throne, but after one special act of mercy and grace, Solomon saw the slimy hand of envy and jealousy attempt to choke and destroy the kingdom. When Adonijah expressed his desire to Bathsheba, Solomon's mother, to take the concubine of David for himself, it was too much. Solomon saw the truth about his own brother. Solomon confronted the problem decisively. He killed Adonijah, and his peaceful reign continued.

Successful people are envied. They are also hated. Does that surprise you? These uncommon achievers are often despised by those who those who want to "climb the ladder to the top."

Donald Trump says, "One of the problems when you become successful is that jealousy and envy inevitably follow. There are people—I call them life's losers who get their sense of accomplishment and achievement from trying to stop others."

You will always have flawed people in your life. Every person has some degree of damage, personal pain and incompetence. Those who work around you may make some mistakes in decision-making and judgment. These mistakes are often the result of misinterpretation of data or trusting the wrong people. So you will have a multitude of *opportunities* to show mercy and graciousness. Kindness is always a good Seed, when it is planted in the *proper* soil.

However, uncommon people must recognize the devastating results of tolerating disloyalty close to them. You see, when you tolerate untruthful, critical and cunning betrayers, *it endangers the progress of the truthful, the caring and the faithful around you.*

Several years ago, I made a difficult decision. I travel a great deal and depend on certain supervisors to solve any problems that arise in the office. Though I was rarely around, I kept hearing reports of disloyalty, disunity and unhappiness. I could not understand it. Though I spent little time at the office, those I worked with on a daily basis seemed quite happy toward me. There was no ill will at all. Yet, the reports persisted.

Then I began to hear that some of my most loyal and faithful associates were considering working in other places. This stunned me. Their dissatisfaction had never been discussed with me personally.

So I began to analyze and interview each person. I discovered six people who were continuously poisoning the others toward me. I was shocked. You see, these six people were the ones to whom I had given the largest bonuses and the best gifts. They were the ones I tried the most to please. Yet they envied the wonderful things that happened to me. They were jealous, envious and competitive. They sowed their critical spirit into precious and wonderful people who were never around me. The Seeds began to grow.

I fired all six in one afternoon.

I wondered what would happen. I knew the workload would increase for the others, but I had no idea who I would hire to replace them. I only understood one thing—*strife cannot be tolerated*. Ever.

It destroys too many good people.

What happened was remarkable. I walked into my office the next day and it felt like Heaven on earth. Those whose countenances had been clouded with uncertainty and fear were happy and joyous. The cloud had lifted. The rainbow had come. Disloyal people are wrong people.

When Wrong People Leave Your Life, Wrong Things Stop Happening.

One of the biggest mistakes of my entire life has been to tolerate wrong people too long. Disloyalty is not like a common cold. You cannot take two aspirins and go to bed. Disloyalty is more like a cancer racing throughout your body.

3 Characteristics of Disloyal People

► Disloyal people do not want you to change. They want you *removed*.

► Disloyal people do not believe they are wrong. They believe *you* are wrong.

► Disloyal people do not pursue *a solution* to the problem. They believe *you* are their problem.

No amount of money can turn a disloyal employee into a loyal one. It is not a money issue. It is a *character* issue.

6 Keys That Will Help You Deal With Disloyalty

1. **Do Not Lie To Yourself About A Disloyal Person.** Be honest and face it with your heart.

2. **Make Certain That All The Facts Can Be Proven Beyond A Shadow of A Doubt.** Gossip is not fact. There are good people whose names have been stained because someone pointed a finger at them. Do not receive every report as truth.

3. **Give The Person Accused Their Right To Be Heard.** Bring in everyone involved. Recently, one of my staff members made a statement to another staff member. I immediately called every person involved into my office. It is usually unwise to listen to an accusation against someone not present. Be sure to have the accused in your presence when the accusation is made.

4. **Ask Sincere And Appropriate Questions of Those You Feel Might Be Disloyal.** Compare their answers with their actions. *Stop reading lips and*

start reading footprints.

    5.   Discuss With The Person The Reasons Why He or She Is Being Fired. Be honest and open, and make it as fair and equitable as possible.

    6.   Make Certain The Terminated Person's Departure Is Conducted With Gentleness, Dignity And Legal Protocol. You can be sued easily if you fail to handle a termination properly. Always consult with your lawyer. Make certain that every penny you owe that person is paid in full. If severance pay is appropriate, it is better to make the sacrifice now than end up with years of ill will sown in your direction.

    Solomon refused to tolerate disloyalty in any way. This is one of the Golden Secrets that helped him become The Richest Man Who Ever Lived.

⤙ 21 ⤚

SOLOMON WAS THANKFUL FOR THE IRREPLACEABLE GIFT OF FAVOR FROM OTHERS

The Wise Always Remember Acts of Kindness.

Kindness is a rare gift to us. Every single act of graciousness is worthy of celebration. This can be a cold, harsh, uncaring world. So, when someone makes a decision to help you get ahead, they deserve to be acknowledged and remembered.

Solomon acted on this principle.

When he contacted Hiram, the king of Tyre, he mentioned the king's relationship with his own father, King David. We read in 2 Chronicles 2:3 that Solomon wrote Hiram, the king of Tyre, these words, "As thou didst deal with David my father, and didst send him cedars to build him an house to dwell therein, even so deal with me."

Solomon's father, King David, wrote many songs of gratitude and thankfulness to God. We can see from his writings that he passed this attitude on to his son.

Solomon had been *mentored* in gratitude.

One Sentence From Solomon Reveals The Following 8 Facts To Hiram:

1.   *You have been the topic of conversation in our palace.*

2.   *My father loved you.*

3.   *Your character and reputation for kindness, giving and generosity have been on the lips of my entire family for years.*

4.   *You are trusted, remembered and celebrated as a friend to those who need a friend.*

5.   *I, too, am thankful that you are accessible and appreciate the opportunity to be connected to you.*

6.   *Your participation in my dream and project is greatly valued.*

7.   *I have something to bring into our relationship that will bless you and help you prosper.*

8.   *You and I belong together.*

I believe that thankfulness is a lost art. I have written scores of generous checks to people over the last thirty-two years of my life. Less than three out of ten wrote back or personally expressed appreciation.

Many years ago, I instituted a rewarding tradition in my life. For the past forty years, I have traveled throughout the world, visiting forty countries. I have made many personal friends whom I value greatly. I think of these people often. However, my hectic schedule often prevents me from communicating with them on a consistent basis.

In response to this, I made a decision to sit down once a year at Thanksgiving and write a personal note of appreciation to each of my friends. I started with the top ten people in my life. Then, I added twenty individuals who had made a profound impact on me.

As my finances increased, I wanted to do something more. Along with my note of appreciation, began sending a smoked turkey to each of the top ten friends on my list. This special gift for their Thanksgiving meal is intended to remind them that I am grateful for their love, support and friendship. The response has been gratifying. Several of my friends have called to say, "You have spoiled us with that smoked turkey every year! We don't even purchase a turkey anymore because we are looking forward to that Mike Murdock turkey."

This is a small gesture compared to what these people have invested in my life. But it is from my heart, and it is tangible evidence of my appreciation. I hope that one day I will be financially able to do this for all my friends. But until that time I am happy to be able to express my gratitude to some of those who have so greatly influenced my life.

Take a moment right now, and make a list of the people you are most thankful for in your life. Call it, "My Thanksgiving List." Your list can include relatives, former mentors or teachers, and those who stood by you with encouragement during specific seasons of crisis.

Be thorough—keep thinking...and thinking...and thinking. Sometimes, those who do the most for us are so close that we overlook them.

Now, *create a complete list of their telephone numbers, fax numbers and addresses.* This is your Thanksgiving Love Circle. Think of creative ways to express your gratitude to them. You might want to telephone them on the first day of each month with a small word of appreciation. You might want to send a two-line, handwritten note of love on the first of each month. Or, you may want to send them a gift of appreciation on Thanksgiving Day as I do.

▶ *To Be Unforgotten, You Must Do Something
Unforgettable.*
▶ *To Be Desired, You Must Become Desirable.*

One of my most wonderful memories is a young
man who kept telling me over and over, "Thank you for
the privilege of letting me work for you. Being around
you is one of the gifts of God for my life." That
registered deep within me.

Who has made the greatest difference in your life?
Who would stand with you if everyone else left? Who
was instrumental in helping you get your present job?

I have been reading a book by Dave Thomas, the
founder of Wendy's International. He was a remarkable
man who showed appreciation for Minnie Sinclair, his
adoptive grandmother, and Frank and George Regas,
his first mentors. Though he was worth millions of
dollars, he had not forgotten to thank Phil Clauss, who
gave him a job at the Hobby House Restaurant when
his family moved to Fort Wayne, Indiana.

Champions are always thankful, especially for
favor.

6 Important Facts Champions Know About Appreciation

1. **Everybody Wants To Be Appreciated.** All
people, no matter how famous or wealthy, wear an
invisible sign around their necks saying, "Please tell me
I'm important to you."

2. **It Only Takes A Moment To Express
Gratitude And Appreciation.** It does not take a
Ph.D., a $20,000 bonus, or two hours of your time.
Sometimes, one simple sentence, a brief phone call, or a

short note will unlock a great river of appreciation.

3. You Do Not Have To Spend A Lot of Money. Graciousness is free. You may be making $5.00 an hour, but what you make doesn't have anything to do with gratitude, thankfulness and appreciation. Even the wealthy do not require expensive gifts—*just thoughtful and sincere words of appreciation.*

4. Never Take Lightly The Favor Others Bestow On Your Life. It is not a small thing in a big world; it is a big thing in a small world.

5. Learn To Speak Words of Gratitude. Every child should be taught the magic and miracle words of hospitality—"Thank you. I appreciate this so much! You have been such a blessing! You have just made things so much easier for me! I can't thank you enough!" *It is impossible to be too thankful in life.*

6. When You Express Gratitude, You Become Remembered Yourself. Thankfulness makes you stand out from the masses. Have you longed for your difference to be observed and noted? Be thankful. Have you longed for your boss to see your significance and respect it? Show gratitude. It's something he probably sees very rarely.

Begin today. Do not put it off another moment. Begin with your family. Express your appreciation for your husband or wife after work today. Speak words of gratefulness to your children when they come in from school today. Start your Thanksgiving Love Circle now. Sow your words of love lavishly, consistently and to every person who is worthy.

Develop a passion for gratitude, thankfulness and appreciation. It is a characteristic of extraordinary and uncommon people.

Proverbs 3:27 says, "Withhold not good from them to whom it is due, when it is in the power of thine hand to do it."

Solomon was thankful for the irreplaceable Gift of Favor from others. He understood the importance of a grateful heart. That is one of the Golden Secrets that helped him become The Richest Man Who Ever Lived.

≈ 22 ≈

SOLOMON TRUSTED
HIS MENTOR

Mentors Are Golden Bridges To Your Future.

Mentors are those who have been where you want to go. They have done something you want to accomplish. Their endurance qualifies them to counsel and advise you.

Solomon makes many references to *"being taught."* The golden thread that runs through all his writings is the importance of "hearing the instructions" of others.

He described those who rebelled against mentorship as *fools,* and those who respected correction as *wise.* In Proverbs 9:9, he says, "Give instruction to a wise man, and he will be yet wiser: teach a just man, and he will increase in learning."

Solomon's father, David was a great psalmist and warrior of Israel. It is almost certain that at some point he shared with Solomon concerning his desire to build the Temple. It is also likely that David confided in Solomon that God had refused him because he was a man of war. It is an uncommon protégé who qualifies to hear in confidentiality the mentor's painful moments. Solomon qualified.

Solomon was proud of the fact that God had spoken about his Assignment to his mentor, King David. He freely addressed it in front of the people.

This was also the case with Samuel, who as a young boy was mentored by the old priest, Eli. God conversed with Samuel and disclosed certain confidential matters with him concerning Eli. *Uncommon mentors recognize the hand of God on uncommon protégés.*

12 Important Keys On Mentorship

1. **Your Mentor Is A Gift From God.** Don't treat him lightly. Celebrate him. Pursue him.

2. **You Will Need To Pursue Your Mentor.** He does not need what you know nearly as much as you need him.

3. **He Does Not Require Your Knowledge, But You Require His.** He has already accomplished his dreams without you. Your dreams are still to be established. Your problems are those he has already solved.

4. **Your Mentor Is Not Your Cheerleader.** He is your coach.

5. **Your Mentor Is Not Present To Confirm What You Are Doing Right, But To Correct You Where You Are Wrong.**

6. **Focus On The Center of Your Mentor's Expertise.** There may be other areas of weakness in your mentor's life. Your lawyer may not be a great cook, so focus on learning *legal* matters from him rather than cooking.

7. **Schedule Private Moments With Your Mentor.** He will act differently to you in private than he will in the presence of others. Something exclusively for you will emerge if you'll take the time.

8. **Keep In Continuous Touch With Your**

Mentor, And Ask Appropriate Questions As They Arise. Keep your notebook handy. When a thought or idea arises, document it. Then discuss it on the telephone or when you meet with him.

9. **Your Mentor Will Usually Only Comment On The Subjects You Ask About.** I have seen those around me make a number of mistakes. My time was too hectic or their interest too low for me to comment effectively. Later, they approached me and shared their failure. I knew it would happen all along. But they were unwilling to pursue information prior to their decisions.

10. **Do Not Share The Trusted Secrets Received From Your Mentor With Just Anyone.** That is what keeps your relationship special. For various reasons, I have heard comments and thoughts from my mentors that I could never share publicly. But those words and comments enabled me to understand more about the humanity of my mentors and the touch of God on their lives.

11. **Recognize That The Humanity of Your Mentor Is There To Be An Encouragement, Not A Distraction.** If your mentor was perfect, he would not be able to tolerate your presence! You see, if you observe extraordinary success from someone obviously flawed, you can draw confidence from them. You, too, can experience unusual success, despite your own weaknesses. It is also helpful to watch what others do wrong, so you can learn from their mistakes.

12. **You Must Be Prepared To Live Your Life Without Your Mentor Present.** David died and Solomon then had to depend upon God completely and totally. *Solomon celebrated the discoveries of others.*

There are people around you who have something that you do not have. Never forget this. Others have experienced events, made observations, and know things you have not yet discovered.

Celebrate their discoveries.

Solomon collected 3,000 proverbs of Wisdom. He retrieved, used and protected the Wisdom of his father, David and many others. At the same time, he embraced new discoveries and perceived additional revelation. He was not a "know-it-all." He reached out to others and recognized their skills, gifts and talents. His dream of building the greatest Temple on earth could not have been realized had he not celebrated the discoveries of others.

Recently, a young man who told everyone that I was his mentor approached me. He kept talking about being my "protégé." So, I decided to put him to a little test.

"You claim to be my protégé. Tell me the last three questions you have asked me."

He looked stunned. He thought...and thought... and thought. He could not recall a single question he had asked me in the previous thirty days, even though he had access to me and had sat by my side in meeting after meeting, hour after hour.

He had never asked me one question.

Stop calling yourself a protégé of someone you never discuss or study anything with. If you make important decisions without the counsel of your mentor, you are not really his or her protégé. If you spend huge amounts of money without asking for counsel from your mentor, you cannot be categorized as a true protégé.

4 Qualities of The Uncommon Protégé

1.   **The Uncommon Protégé Celebrates The Discoveries of His Mentors.**

2.   **The Uncommon Protégé Recognizes His Need To Change.** If you fail to recognize your need for change, you will never pursue change. You will not appreciate those around you who require it and urge you toward it.

3.   **The Uncommon Protégé Trusts His Mentor.** He is willing to consider his instructions whether he understands them or not. Elisha did this when Elijah told him, "If you see me when I'm taken, you will receive the double portion." Elisha may have not known what that meant, but he trusted his mentor.

Ruth trusted Naomi when she suggested she visit the home of Boaz. Ruth seemed very contented as a single woman. But she listened carefully to the words of her mentor.

A protégé who refuses to follow the instructions of his mentor, is indicating that he does not completely trust his mentor's counsel. This is a dangerous season for a protégé. The Seed of uncertainty will eventually lead to division and criticism of his mentor. Every time I have seen habitual and flagrant disregard for my instructions, I have watched a critical spirit develop in my protégé.

4.   **The Uncommon Protégé Knows That When He Stops Asking, The Mentor Stops Answering.** Mentors often wait to be asked and they know many things that they never discuss. It is only when the protégé asks that the answers begin to flow.

This happened in the life of Jesus. *He knew many*

things but not until the disciples asked did He begin to answer. The Ethiopian eunuch had a need, but it was only when he asked Philip to join him that he received Philip's help. (See Acts 8.)

Solomon was an uncommon protégé. He trusted his mentor. He understood that this is one of the Golden Secrets that helped him become The Richest Man Who Ever Lived.

≈ 23 ≈

SOLOMON LEARNED FROM HIS TRAGEDIES

Tragedies Happen To Almost Everyone.

The poor often feel targeted and singled out for catastrophe. In their hearts, they sometimes believe money can solve any problem. But the rich also cry and have sleepless nights. The wealthy are not exempt from pain.

Look at the life of Solomon. Tragedies were woven through the fabric of his life like a horrible crimson thread.

His father, David, murdered his mother's first husband. I am certain the entire family had a thousand conversations about the horrifying scheme and conspiracy to have Uriah killed in battle. Solomon's sister was raped by one of his brothers. Another brother, Absalom, attempted to destroy his father and his rule. Solomon's own brother tried to wrestle the kingship from him.

Yet, somehow, he kept his focus. He fought for it. *He believed in his own destiny.*

He saw *beyond* his tragedies.

He saw the golden rewards of *persistence.*

Persistence is not a chosen quality. It is produced by an obsession. Such determination can only come from a total focus on something you desire.

Solomon knew this. As these words written in Ecclesiastes explain, [There is] "A time to love, and a time to hate...a time to break down, and a time to build up," (Ecclesiastes 3:8, 3). He embraced each season, learned from each, and gained Wisdom from each.

The successful cannot always prevent a tragedy *around* them, but they can prevent it from becoming a tragedy *within* them.

Great men have known great pain.

We all hurt with Bill Cosby, the beloved comedian, when his son, Ennis, was found murdered on the side of the road. Bill Cosby epitomizes common sense and stability. How did this remarkably wealthy and successful entertainer cope with the death of his only son? He phoned the mother of a girl murdered in a drive-by shooting on the same day his son died! He encouraged and comforted *her.*

Bill Cosby coped with his loss by expressing gratitude that he had been able to enjoy his son for the years he was here. Then he reached out to comfort somebody else who was hurting. *What You Make Happen For Others, God Will Make Happen For You.*

Mary Kay Ash planned her business with excitement. Then, just before opening, her husband died suddenly. It was catastrophic. He was a major part of her life and a great help to her. Suddenly he was *gone*—in the middle of the biggest dream of her life.

She did not quit. Certainly she fought back the tears of pain, disappointment and disillusionment. But she went back to the dream within her. She acknowledged that her life was a long way from over. Her son joined her in her great achievement to help women succeed in their own business. It worked. Today thousands of women have been motivated, restored and blessed because of this extraordinary and uncommon woman.

Comedian Bill Cosby and famed businesswoman Mary Kay Ash have this in common: they have faced their tragedies and conquered.

Your dream must go on.

Your goals must continue to be fed within you.

You may experience waves of pain more devastating than you could ever imagine. The person you love most may betray you. Your children may refuse to visit you. Your father may never say a kind word to your face. You may not even know your father or mother. The circumstances of your life may be unfortunate beyond description.

But that is not the reason to fail or quit.

Read the incredible story of Dave Thomas, the legendary founder of Wendy's International. On page 31 of his book, *Well Done,* we learn that he too experienced emptiness and loneliness as a child. You, also, can overcome any tragedy.

7 Important Keys To Remember In Painful Seasons

1. You Cannot Prevent Every Tragedy From Occurring, But You Can Prevent It From Destroying You.

2. Your Future Is Too Wonderful To Stop. Put your energy and focus on something in front of you, not behind you.

3. The Broken Often Become Masters At Mending. When you experience inner pain, you have an opportunity to become the golden key of healing for somebody else who is hurting. Look around. Permit your own tragedy to soften your heart and make you a healer to the hurting around you.

4.   Those Who Unlock Your Compassion Are Those To Whom You Have Been Assigned. When someone around you stirs up your heart of caring, pay attention to it. That usually is a Golden Link to your future.

5.   Do Not Keep Asking The Wrong Questions. Instead of "why?" ask, "What is my *next* step toward my dream?" When you ask the right questions, the right answers emerge.

6.   Give Yourself Time To Heal.

7.   Do Not Rush Away From The Scene of Pain. There is a lot to *learn* and a lot to *feel*. A funeral often births regret, but regret births changes. Change can bring great joy to others.

I will never forget when a mother standing over the casket of her child said, "I now will enjoy my children who are left with me more than ever. I had no idea this would happen so quickly, and I could lose them." She told me later that she realized 99 percent of all the arguments and quarrels she had with her children were totally unnecessary. She placed too much emphasis on conflict, rather than focusing on conversation and enjoyment.

When you suffer a loss or a tragedy, take time out to look through the bookstore and find experiences of others who have encountered what you are going through. If the doctor has told you your disease is incurable, begin to listen to testimonies and reflect on the victories of those who have received supernatural healing. Work to build up your faith. Pour yourself into your future.

Your future is too good to be ignored.

Solomon *learned from tragedy.* It is one of the Golden Secrets that helped him become The Richest Man Who Ever Lived.

What You Hear
Determines
What You Feel.

-MIKE MURDOCK

≈ 24 ≈

SOLOMON UNDERSTOOD THE DEVASTATING EFFECT OF WRONG WORDS

Words Can Create Life or Death Around Us.

No one on earth understood the power of a single word like Solomon. He collected 3,000 proverbs and wrote 1,005 songs.

Solomon also understood the effect that words have on others. In 1 Kings 5:4, he says, "But now the Lord my God hath given me rest on every side, so that there is neither adversary nor evil occurrent."

He did not say, "This is too good to be true. I'm expecting an enemy to rise up at any time against me." Solomon continuously painted the portrait of peace and prosperity with his words.

He did not discuss his doubts with everyone.

His words did not inject the atmosphere and climate with fear of anticipated distraction and loss.

Those who came into Solomon's presence heard comforting, encouraging, uplifting words.

That is precisely why people came from everywhere to speak with him. Their own fears, unbelief and anxiety had poisoned their lives. *They craved to be in the presence of someone who could see a great future.*

Television is filled with psychics, fortune-tellers and those who say they can predict your future. Millions of people pursue astrologers. And millions of dollars are spent in pursuit of those who can tell us something good is going to happen in our lives. This is one of the Master Secrets of successful men.

Solomon used words as *bridges,* helping people move from where they were to where their dreams were.

Solomon used words as *exits* from the present so they could move away from the troubles in their lives. He knew that right words always blessed people.

What Solomon said made people happy. The queen of Sheba commented on this in 1 Kings 10:8, "Happy are thy men, happy are these thy servants, which stand continually before thee, and that hear thy Wisdom." She discovered something few others learn.

What You Hear Determines What You Feel. The following proverbs have the power to change your life forever. I encourage you to memorize them. They have come from the heart of The Richest Man Who Ever Lived.

▶ "Hear; for I will speak of excellent things; and the opening of my lips shall be right things," (Proverbs 8:6).

▶ "The mouth of the righteous man is a well of life," (Proverbs 10:11).

▶ "Whoso keepeth his mouth and his tongue keepeth his soul from troubles," (Proverbs 21:23).

Solomon Taught The Following 47 Facts About Words

1.   **Words Can Poison And Destroy A Young Man's Entire Life.** (Read Proverbs 7.)

2.   **Right Advice Guaranteed Safety And Protection.** "In the multitude of counsellors, there is safety," (Proverbs 11:14).

3.   **Any Man Who Controls His Mouth Is Literally Protecting His Own Life.** "He that keepeth his mouth keepeth his life," (Proverbs 13:3).

4.   **Those Who Talk Too Much Will Eventually Be Destroyed.** "He that openeth wide his lips shall have destruction," (Proverbs 13:3).

5.   **Right Words Can Turn An Angry Man Into A Friend, And Wrong Words Can Turn A Friend Into An Enemy.** "A soft answer turneth away wrath: but grievous words stir up anger," (Proverbs 15:1).

6.   **Your Words Reveal Whether You Are Wise or A Fool.** "The tongue of the wise useth knowledge aright: but the mouth of fools poureth out foolishness," (Proverbs 15:2).

7.   **Right Words Breathe Life Into Everything Around You.** "A wholesome tongue is a tree of life," (Proverbs 15:4).

8.   **The Purpose of Words Is To Educate, Enthuse And Enlarge Those Around You.** "The lips of the wise disperse knowledge," (Proverbs 15:7).

9.   **Your Personal Happiness Is Influenced By The Words That Come Out of Your Own Mouth.** "A man hath joy by the answer of his mouth: and a word spoken in due season, how good is it!" (Proverbs 15:23).

10. The Wise Are Cautious With Their Words. "He that hath knowledge spareth his words," (Proverbs 17:27).

11. Right Words Are As Important As Water On Earth And The Sustaining of Human Life. "The words of a man's mouth are as deep waters, and the wellspring of Wisdom as a flowing brook," (Proverbs 18:4).

12. Men Fail Because of The Words They Speak. "A fools mouth is his destruction, and his lips are the snare of his soul," (Proverbs 18:7).

13. Wrong Words Wound Others And Destroy People And Friendships Forever. "The words of a talebearer are as wounds, and they go down into the innermost parts of the belly," (Proverbs 18:8).

14. Words Determine Which Dreams Live or Die. "Death and life are in the power of the tongue: and they that love it shall eat the fruit thereof," (Proverbs 18:21).

15. Any Words You Allow Others To Speak Into You Is Deciding The Wisdom You Contain. "Hear counsel, and receive instruction, that thou mayest be wise in thy latter end," (Proverbs 19:20). Solomon knew that words were the difference between his present season and his future season.

16. Wrong Words Are The Reason Men Fall Into Error. "Cease, my son, to hear the instruction that causeth to err from the words of knowledge," (Proverbs 19:27).

17. Good Men Study Their Words Before They Speak Them. "The heart of the righteous studieth to answer," (Proverbs 15:28).

18. The Tongue Is The Major Cause of All

Troubles. "Whoso keepeth his mouth and his tongue keepeth his soul from troubles," (Proverbs 21:23).

19. Fools Seldom Understand The Power of Words. "Speak not in the ears of a fool: for he will despise the Wisdom of thy words," (Proverbs 23:9).

20. Talking To Fools Is A Waste of Time. "Speak not in the ears of a fool: for he will despise the Wisdom of thy words," (Proverbs 23:9).

21. Wisdom Is A Result of The Words You Hear. "Hear thou, my son, and be wise," (Proverbs 23:19).

22. The Timing of Your Words Often Decides Your Success or Failure In A Situation. "A fool uttereth all his mind: but a wise man keepeth it in till afterwards," (Proverbs 29:11).

23. Influential People Should Use Their Words And Influence To Help The Poor And Needy. "Open thy mouth, judge righteously, and plead the cause of the poor and needy," (Proverbs 31:9).

24. The Words of Wise Women Are Consistently Kind. "She openeth her mouth with Wisdom; and in her tongue is the law of kindness," (Proverbs 31:26).

25. Your Words Can Become The Trap That Destroys You. "Thou art snared with the words of thy mouth," (Proverbs 6:2).

26. Right Words Feed And Sustain Those Around You. "The lips of the righteous feed many: but fools die for want of Wisdom," (Proverbs 10:21).

27. Right Words Are As Important As Silver And Gold. "The tongue of the just is as choice silver," (Proverbs 10:20).

28. Right Words Can Get You Out of Any

Difficulty And Trouble. "The mouth of the upright shall deliver them," (Proverbs 12:6).

29. Right Words Bring Health And Healing. "The tongue of the wise is health," (Proverbs 12:18).

30. The Wise Avoid The Presence of Those Who Consistently Speak Wrong Words. "Go from the presence of a foolish man, when thou perceivest not in him the lips of knowledge," (Proverbs 14:7).

31. Only The Simple And Fools Believe Everything Others Say. "The simple believeth every word: but the prudent man looketh well to his going," (Proverbs 14:15).

32. Right Words Give You Access To Powerful And Important People. "Righteous lips are the delight of kings; and they love him that speaketh right," (Proverbs 16:13).

33. Wisdom Is Necessary In Order To Speak The Right Words. "The heart of the wise teacheth his mouth, and addeth learning to his lips," (Proverbs 16:23).

34. Pleasant Words Are The Sweetest Sounds On Earth. "Pleasant words are as an honeycomb, sweet to the soul, and health to the bones," (Proverbs 16:24).

35. The Sweetness of Right Words Could Help To Cure Any Bitterness Existent In The Human Soul. "Pleasant words are as an honeycomb, sweet to the soul, and health to the bones," (Proverbs 16:24).

36. The Quality of Your Words Reveals The Quality of Your Heart. "An ungodly man diggeth up evil: and in his lips there is as a burning fire," (Proverbs 16:27). You can read the heart of any person by listening to the words they are speaking about others.

37. Words Will Quickly Expose Envy And Jealousy or Admiration And Respect. "An ungodly man diggeth up evil: and in his lips there is as a burning fire," (Proverbs 16:27).

38. The Greatest Friendships On Earth Are Broken Because of Wrong Words. "A whisperer separateth chief friends," (Proverbs 16:28).

39. Strife Can Always Be Traced To Someone's Words. "A froward man soweth strife," (Proverbs 16:28).

40. Evil Is Released Through The Lips. "Moving his lips he bringeth evil to pass," (Proverbs 16:30).

41. You Should Not Answer Anything Until You Have Heard All The Details. "He that answereth a matter before he heareth it, it is folly and shame unto him," (Proverbs 18:13). Accuracy is only important when adequate information is available.

42. Words Influence And Affect The Accumulation of Your Wealth. "A man's belly shall be satisfied with the fruit of his mouth; and with the increase of his lips shall he be filled," (Proverbs 18:20). This is almost never mentioned in prosperity teaching today. Yet using the wrong words can get you fired or prevent you from getting promoted.

I remember times I was going to give someone a raise until I brought them in and heard the words they were speaking. Complaining, blaming, fault-finding words can stop a boss from promoting you.

43. Right Words Can Release A Boss To Promote You or Give You A Raise. "A man's belly shall be satisfied with the fruit of his mouth; and with the increase of his lips shall he be filled," (Proverbs 18:20).

44. One Conversation With The Wrong Woman Can Destroy Your Life. "The mouth of strange women is a deep pit: he that is abhorred of the Lord shall fall therein," (Proverbs 22:14).

45. Never Enter Into Battle Without Sufficient Counsel. "For by wise counsel thou shalt make thy war: and in multitude of counsellors there is safety," (Proverbs 24:6).

46. The Wise Avoid "Self-Praise." "Let another man praise thee, and not thine own mouth; a stranger, and not thine own lips," (Proverbs 27:2).

47. Lying Words Can Poison The Attitude of A Boss Toward An Employee. "If a ruler hearken to lies, all his servants are wicked," (Proverbs 29:12).

Dave Thomas was the famous founder of Wendy's International. On page 136 of his book, *Well Done,* he made a powerful statement: "Today, communication is the heart of success." I encourage you to read this excellent book!

Solomon understood the remarkable power of words. That is one of the Golden Secrets that helped him become The Richest Man Who Ever Lived.

～ 25 ～

SOLOMON NEVER WASTED TIME CORRECTING FOOLS

Fools Are Everywhere.

Correcting them is physically exhausting. It breaks your focus and wastes valuable time and energy.

Former President Richard Nixon once commented on Lee Iacocca, the legendary leader of Chrysler, that he had one major problem—no tolerance for fools. Nixon further explained that his attitude created two more problems! First, there are so many fools, and second, some people that you think are fools really are not!

One of my favorite people is Dexter Yager, the beloved champion in the Amway business. He is a hero to millions. In his excellent book, *Don't Let Anyone Steal Your Dream,* he writes, "There are three classes of people: losers, leaners, and leaders." I agree, and it is vital to discern the difference.

Solomon understood the futility of correcting fools. He refused to educate them, motivate them or associate with them. *He even avoided conversation with them.* Proverbs 26:4 says, "Answer not a fool according to his folly, lest thou also be like unto him." Solomon simply refused to enter into any relationship with fools. He believed that they should not be given any place of authority, position or honor.

7 Characteristics of Fools

1. Fools Perpetuate To Others Offenses Made Against Them. They want others to feel their pain. They seek to create an army of protestors against the person who offends them, rather than exhibiting a willingness to settle the offense. They will discuss it in their living room, on the telephone and with every friend they meet.

Ahab, for example, was the king, yet he was envious of a vineyard belonging to another man. He responded by stirring up anger in his wife. She had the man killed in order to secure the vineyard. God saw their foolishness and reacted with swift judgment.

2. Fools Want Something They Have Not Earned. Ahab's wife, Queen Jezebel, was also a fool. Her husband's bitter words concerning the man with the vineyard incited murder in her heart. Why? Because Jezebel wanted that which she had not earned.

Several years ago a young man on my staff approached me and asked why he had not received a raise. I pulled a sheet of paper from my notebook.

"Here are the things I have asked you to do numerous times. You still have not completed my previous instructions. Yet I have paid your weekly salary every week. How dare you ask me for more money when you have not yet earned *what I've already paid you.*" He got the point and apologized.

3. Fools Ignore The Counsel of Proven Mentors. God always arranges a wise and experienced person near someone who is inexperienced. That person represents escape from your present and a golden door to your future. Yet every day fools ignore the proven counsel of successful people around them; consequently, their lives are a parade of failures.

4. Fools Refuse To Admit Their Mistakes Even When Their Pain Is The Obvious Proof. Making a mistake does not make you a fool. Refusing to admit it reveals you are a fool.

5. Fools Refuse To Reach For Counsel From Accessible Champions. Recently, I heard a continuous stream of complaints over financial problems. Several around me, it seemed, were upset about their inability to pay bills, and so forth. So, I invested $20,000 and brought six multimillionaires for a special three-day conference. I called it, "The Uncommon Millionaires Conference."

Each and every person who had been complaining about finances had *access* to those extraordinary men for three days. It shocked me when those who were complaining the loudest never showed up for the sessions even though most of them lived less than five minutes from the conference itself. Ignoring available Wisdom is proof of a deep-rooted problem. Certainly, it is characteristic of a fool.

6. Fools Confuse Their Greatest Friends With Their Enemies. In the New Testament, we read that Judas betrayed Christ, yet Jesus Christ was the One who loved him more than anyone else. Children are often influenced by those who offer them drugs instead of their own parents who have provided them with food, clothing and shelter. For the young, this is called the burden of immaturity. For those who are older and should know better, this behavior is called foolish. Who are the *proven* friends in your life? *Never Permit The Untested Acquaintance To Stain The Loyalty of A Proven Friend.*

7.   Fools Often Betray The Ones Who Believe In Them The Most. Someone in this world believes in you. Someone helps you and speaks encouraging words to you; yet thousands do not recognize or appreciate the people in their lives who really care. George Foreman, the famous boxer, is one of my favorite people. He has written an interesting book that I would recommend entitled, *By George.* "Whatever problems my folks had together, it did not affect my father's faith in me. He believed from the time I was an infant that I was going to be a champion. He loved me. He'd never seen my kind of fire in any kid. Like the others, he pushed my buttons to get a rise. Sure enough, I'd go off popping him in the eye.

'Heavyweight champion of the world,' he'd shout, raise my arm after I'd tried to beat up someone four times my size. 'Stronger than Jack Johnson. Hits like Jack Dempsey.'" George Foreman recognized his father as a force of encouragement. George Foreman is not a fool.

Who has invested time in *correcting* you? *Mentoring* you?   Pouring encouragement into you? *Invest yourself in them in return.* Protect them as a gift from God in your life.

Never waste your energy on fools. This is one of the Golden Secrets that helped Solomon become The Richest Man Who Ever Lived.

❧ 26 ❧

SOLOMON REWARDED THOSE WHO HELPED HIM ACHIEVE HIS GOAL

Reward Those Who Solve Problems For You.

You will never achieve any significant dream without others who care about you and want to be a part of your life.

Hiram, the king of Tyre, assisted Solomon by providing workers and servants. Though there is some controversy about how those workers were compensated under Solomon, the ancient writings document the following in 1 Kings 5:11, "And Solomon gave Hiram twenty thousand measures of wheat for food to his household, and twenty measures of pure oil: thus gave Solomon to Hiram year by year." In other words, Solomon paid his workers an agreeable salary.

6 Keys In Rewarding Your Love Circle

1. Reward Your Family When They Help You Achieve Your Goal. Many years ago, my father did something that I will never forget. The largest salary any church ever paid my father as pastor was $125 each week. From that meager wage, he fed, clothed, and sheltered his wife and seven children. He even paid rent on the parsonage we lived in. One evening, he presented us with a very unusual challenge.

"Kids, I want to show you our electricity bill last month. It is really important that each of you turn the lights off when you leave a room or close the closet door. Let's keep the air conditioners turned off a little more. In fact, mother and I want to do something very special for you children if you will help us out on this. We have agreed to take the difference between this light bill and the one that will arrive in thirty days and take you out for ice cream. You can have all you want, depending on how much is saved."

His challenge excited us beyond words.

I do not have many memories of ice cream and those types of goodies. It was a wonderful occasion and an opportunity to be blessed. So for the next thirty days, each of us challenged the others. "You forgot to turn your light off!" was a scream often heard through the house.

It had never mattered to us before. Regardless of how many times Daddy told us to turn off the lights, when he wasn't around, they stayed on. Suddenly, our conduct and behavior was the very opposite. Why? *The reward.*

There was something in it for us. Selfish? Not at all.

> ▶ *Self-care* is doing something that benefits yourself.
> ▶ *Selfishness* is *depriving another* of something to advantage and benefit yourself.

The light bill came down because Daddy decided to reward us for assisting him in his goal.

2. Uncommon Achievers Always Want To

Understand The Rewards They Will Receive For Solving A Problem. I love the electrifying story of David, the shepherd boy. According to the Old Testament, he single-handedly killed a lion and a bear.

When David brought the lunch to his brothers in battle, he saw and heard the screaming and cursing of Goliath, the great Philistine giant.

Do you remember the first thing he did? He asked what the *rewards* would be for the man who killed the giant. Somebody told him that he would be able to marry the king's daughter and never pay taxes the rest of his life. *That reward birthed uncommon desire within him.*

He ran to the brook and secured five stones. When he returned, he yelled out to the giant, "Your head is coming off!" And it did!

3.   Continuously Paint The Portrait of Reward In The Minds of Those Who Share Your Vision. Sometimes, it is wise to *remind* those around you about the rewards. *You* may think about them daily, but they may not. Their minds are often filled with the toils, burdens and tears of their own lives.

4.   Sometimes You Have To Remind Yourself of The Rewards of Your Own Goals And Dreams. It is not always easy to remember the reasons you are pursuing your goals.

The pain of the present often blurs the potential of the future. Don't get sidetracked and distracted. Stop often and evaluate the results of your efforts. Why are you doing what you are doing? Think for a moment. Have you ever forgotten the picture of financial independence and success? Of course you have. Have you ever thought you would be sick forever? Of course.

Someone had to remind you that the best is yet ahead.

Solomon constantly painted the *portrait of prosperity* to his people.

That is why the Queen of Sheba commented on "...the happiness of those who work around you."

You are continuously educating your *staff.*

You are continuously educating your *family.*

You are continuously reminding *yourself* why you are doing what you are doing.

5. Reward Your Leaders Relative To The Problems They Solve. Peter J. Daniels, one of my favorite speakers, addressed hundreds of ministers at the Mabee Center in Tulsa, Oklahoma, some months ago. He explained how each minister should be totally focused on his personal spiritual life of prayer and study. He encouraged every minister to hire another leader who would assume all responsibility for the office staff, financial records and legalities. He felt that every minister should invest his life in spiritual ministry only. Every one of us felt like shouting out, "Yes!"

Then, he added with a twinkle in his eye, "Just remember to pay that person the same salary you are paying yourself."

Few are willing to do that.

6. Sow Unexpected Gifts As "Seeds of Appreciation" Into Your Love Circle. Solomon knew how to reward other people. Listen to his comments about gifts taken from Proverbs 29:4 and 19:6, "The king by judgment establisheth the land: but he that receiveth gifts overthroweth it." "Many will intreat the favour of the prince: and every man is a friend to him that giveth gifts."

Luke 10:7 says, "The labourer is worthy of his hire."

One of the strongest teachings in Scripture is the hatred God has for injustice and unfair treatment. Proverbs 11:1 says, "A false balance is abomination to the Lord: but a just weight is his delight."

Solomon knew that diligence would be rewarded with prosperity and provision and good pay: "The diligent tend only to plenteousness," (Proverbs 21:5).

Sam Walton, the legendary billionaire, knew this principle very well. He refused to call his workers "employees." In fact, he loved calling them his "associates." They felt rewarded and honored to be a part of every success.

4 Powerful Questions Every Visionary Must Ask Himself

1.   **What Role Do Those Around You Play In The Achievement of Your Goals And Dreams?**
2.   **Have You Written Out Your *Expectations* For Those Around You In Clearly Defined Terms?**
3.   **Are Those Around You Comfortable And Knowledgeable And *Agreeable* With Your Responsibilities For *Them*?**
4.   **What Are The Rewards For Those Who Help You Reach Your Publicized Goal And Dream?** A few years ago, I walked into a telethon studio and found a disheartened and demoralized group of people. Every phone was dead. No one was calling. The volunteers were crying, yelling and screaming at the people "in television land." Still, nobody would call.

After watching for a few minutes, I asked the

young leader, "What are you wanting the people to do?"

He looked shocked. "Well, anything they feel like doing!"

"That's exactly what they are doing," I answered. "They don't feel like calling, so they are not calling."

"But we need for them to call and make pledges!"

I responded with this simple question, "What will they get out of it by calling?"

His reply was a sincere one. "Well, we will go off the air if they don't call."

I was very direct. "Did they *ask you* to go on the air?"

He looked disheartened, so I quickly explained.

"The members of your audience are morally obligated to move away from anything that decreases them in any way. You have not shown them how participation will *benefit* their lives. Until you do, they are right in refusing to call. Birthing this television program was your idea, not theirs. Let them know what is really in it for them if they call and become a part of your life."

A few moments later, I sat down and shared a few important truths. As I shared those truths with the viewers, the phones began to light up. Within thirty minutes they were jammed—all because the viewers now understood the importance of the program to their own lives.

Always reward those who solve problems for you. Solomon understood this Golden Secret and it helped him become The Richest Man Who Ever Lived.

～ 27 ～

SOLOMON ESTABLISHED A REPUTATION FOR WISDOM AND INTEGRITY

Integrity Attracts Worthy Relationships.

Proven leaders and kings were comfortable with Solomon's integrity, honesty and trustworthiness. In 2 Chronicles 2:12, we read these words of Hiram, the King of Tyre, "Moreover, Blessed be the Lord God of Israel, that made Heaven and earth, who hath given to David the king a wise son, endued with prudence and understanding, that might build an house for the Lord, and an house for his kingdom."

People talk. They talk about your weaknesses, your strengths, your failures, your successes, your fears and your potential. Whether you like it or not, people will form opinions about you.

Your reputation determines the quality of people you attract. Those who are comfortable with your weaknesses will enter your life to continue nurturing those same problems. Those comfortable with your strengths will want to participate in your successes.

Your reputation determines the flow of favor. Everyone loves to participate in the birthing of a success. Once your success is known, everyone will want to participate and become involved. But when your reputation is stained and questionable, quality people withdraw.

It is impossible to overestimate the influence of a good reputation. Solomon fully recognized this and wrote in Proverbs 22:1, "A good name is rather to be chosen than great riches, and loving favour rather than silver and gold."

Wealth cannot purchase worthy relationships. However, worthy friendships always produce wealth in some form. Years ago, I had a conversation with Bob Hope's public relations manager. The famous and much loved comedian has been a companion to presidents and created a favorable reputation around the world. His manager said, "Mike, Bob has *credibility* with people. Two things create credibility. They are *trustworthiness* and *expertise.*"

Trustworthiness demonstrates that you are what you *appear* to be.

Expertise demonstrates that you are the *best* at what you do.

The following two powerful ingredients are necessary to create a good reputation with others. They are simple, yet profound:

1. **Do What You Say You Will Do.** *Pay* the bill you promised to pay. *Finish* what you start.

2. **Do *Quality* Work.**

These two keys create a powerful reputation that attract the right people, uncommon blessing, favor and uncommon financial reward.

Who really believes in you? Why do they believe in you? What are you doing that would disappoint them if they discovered it? What product have you produced that attracts others?

5 Keys That Will Help You Build A High Quality Reputation

1. Establish Achievable Goals With Reasonable Deadlines. Many people ruin their good name because they attempt to please others by agreeing to unreasonable goals and deadlines. You must allow for the unexpected. Setbacks occur. Bad weather. Perhaps you thought a product would be available when it was not. Carefully think through all the potential difficulties you might encounter when considering a job for another person.

Recently, a good man was doing work for me at my house. But he kept adding to the price of his projects. After a few months, I realized that his credibility with me was slipping. I did not believe anything he said anymore. I still feel he has a good heart, but he had not taken time to anticipate the problems associated with the job.

2. Keep Your Promises. Do what you promise others you will do, no matter how much it costs.

3. Develop Quality Friendships Around You. You will be known by the kinds of friends you keep. Your friends reveal the atmosphere your nature requires.

4. Never Sell A Product You Don't Personally Use. Mary Kay Ash, the founder of Mary Kay Cosmetics, Inc., started her company in 1963. Today, it boasts more than 400,000 representatives worldwide and generates retail sales in excess of $2 billion. Mary Kay's representatives are successful because they personally use the products.

On page 23 of the April, 1996 issue of "Business

Startups," an article by Sandra Mardenfeld states, "When you're trying to sell a product, people can tell if you are not really sold on it yourself."

5. Solve The Problems Closest To You. Don't wait until you get a more "important job."

Recorded in the Old Testament is the story of a young man named Joseph, who was able to accurately interpret dreams. Though he was in prison for something he did not do, he interpreted the dreams of two men who were in prison with him. One of the men, a butler, was vindicated and returned to his job in Pharaoh's palace. When the Pharaoh began to have a troubling, recurring dream, the butler recommended that Joseph be brought from prison to interpret the dream. Soon his talents caused him to become the second most powerful individual in Egypt. This happened because Joseph was willing to help those who were close by, even in prison.

During your lifetime, you will be known either as:

▶ The kind of person who *solves* problems for others.

▶ The kind of person who *creates* problems for others.

One day, a friend of mine asked about a gifted young man who had been working with me in my ministry. He asked what kind of employee the man had been and then asked if I would mind if he hired him. You see, this young man received new opportunities because others noted his diligence on my behalf. When it becomes known that you are someone who helps others solve their problems, you will be sought after.

It is also important to honor the "Chain of Credibility." Most pastors ask their secretaries to screen their calls. Therefore, when I contact pastors, I understand that my attitude toward those secretaries will greatly affect their opinion of me and, in many cases, determine whether or not that pastor looks on me with favor. This is the "Chain of Credibility" I must respect to be effective.

Recently, I was told that an acquaintance had been rude to several members of my staff. They reported to me that his behavior had been obnoxious, rude and disheartening. This person lost credibility with me. Why? Because I respect and trust my staff. After all, they are pouring 50 percent of their lives into my vision and life each day. Their time and hard work matters to me. Their words affect me and their opinions are important to me. I do not respect those who are patronizing and loving to my face yet mistreat my staff. They are not honoring the "Chain of Credibility."

You must also honor the "Chain of Authority." Those who have been placed by God in authority over your life are the same people God chooses to *promote* you.

4 Keys In Protecting Your Chain of Promotion

1. **Treasure The Respect Your Parents Give You.** Honor them. Do not fail to nurture and strengthen that relationship with them.

2. **Honor The Spiritual Authority Over Your Life.** Your pastor or spiritual advisor is an important person in the eyes of God. Pursue his or her counsel during crisis times, and always allow that person to speak into your life. Doing this will help you

establish and maintain your good reputation.

3.   **Respect Your Boss.** He or she is receiving a constant report about your life. Be sure that when those around you speak the truth, they are saying things you want your boss to hear.

4.   **Protect Your Reputation.** It determines the flow of favor in your life. Establish a reputation of Wisdom and integrity and you will succeed beyond your wildest dreams.

Solomon knew that reputation matters. That's one of the Golden Secrets that helped him become The Richest Man Who Ever Lived.

⇜ 28 ⇝

SOLOMON UNDERSTOOD THE POWER OF MUSIC

Music Controls The Climate Around You.

Hollywood movie producers will spend almost any amount of money for songs, musicians, and arrangements that will create the best possible atmosphere and mood for their motion pictures. Why? *Because a movie's success greatly depends on the quality of the music in it.*

Around the world, billions of dollars are spent on music cassettes, CD's, and television and stereo entertainment centers. People who lack the finances to put their children through college will invest thousands of dollars to provide music for their homes, offices and cars.

Music *energizes.*

Music *motivates.*

Music *takes us away from the present.*

Music *focuses our hearts on beauty.*

Music *helps us escape* unpleasant circumstances.

Music *heals.*

Music *births hope* for changes in our relationships.

Music *lives* when everything around us is dying.

Music is a *current in the ocean of life* moving us toward the palace of our dreams.

Music *restores* when we have been wounded.

Music *lifts* when crisis thrusts us into a pit.

Music *gives us wings* when tragedy would drag us into a pit of despair.

Music *changes our mind world* within seconds.

Solomon was a king buried knee deep in bureaucracy. Real estate contracts were stacked all over the rooms of his palace. Appointments were scheduled continuously with legislators and leaders. He carried the burden of hospitality when foreign travelers entered his palace, and his family, wives, and friends pulled on him every single day of his life.

But, Solomon never became too busy for his music. It was his life.

In 1 Kings 4:32, we read, "His songs were a thousand and five."

One of the most famous books of the Holy Bible is called the "Song of Solomon" in which he records his romance with the love of his life.

Solomon enjoyed the music of many. Ecclesiastes 2:8 says, "I gat me men singers and women singers, and the delights of the sons of men, as musical instruments, and that of all sorts."

Music is a *tool* that carefully rebuilds the atmosphere of expectation, hope and enthusiasm.

Music is a *weapon* that forces the enemies of fatigue and boredom to be dispelled quickly and instantly from your life.

Music is the *vehicle* that transports you instantly from the valley of depression to the city of creativity.

Music is a *Seed* that grows the "Garden of Greatness" around you rather than the dark forest of human expectations.

Music is the *escape route* when 10,000 tasks race

toward your castle of privacy, seeking to overthrow the throne of tranquillity.

Music is the gate to a supernatural world where the imagination can create any dream you have ever desired.

4 Helpful Keys That Will Help You Design The World of Music Around You

1. **Browse Through Your Local Music Store.** Take the time. Make the investment. You are creating a dream world for your emotions, energy and goals.

2. **Select The Songs That Inspire, Motivate And Strengthen Your Confidence.** Others may not feel what you feel. Your family may not like your music. But, when a song energizes you and brings enthusiasm and faith, it is worth any investment of time or finances.

3. **Ask Those You Admire What Kind of Music Has Inspired Their Imagination.** Everyone has a different taste in music, but you will get some wonderful ideas from these discussions with them.

4. **Invest In The Highest Quality Stereo Equipment For Your Home And Grounds.** I have twenty-four speakers on the trees at my house. I cannot describe to you the wonderful atmosphere when I walk across my seven-acre yard hearing the beautiful songs that generate a supernatural presence and atmosphere around me. It is my world. I have determined my own surroundings. You must learn to do the same.

Solomon understood the powerful influence of music. This is one of the Golden Secrets that helped him become The Richest Man Who Ever Lived.

Those Who Disrespect
Your Assignment,
Are Disqualified
For Relationship.

-MIKE MURDOCK

⇜ 29 ⇝

Solomon Qualified Those Who Had Access To Him

———————◄►○◄—————————

Confidentiality Is Important To The Wealthy.

In fact, confidentiality is *required* among the wealthy because they know that personal information is often distorted, misused, and even sold to the highest bidder. It is not uncommon for the wealthy to ask employees to sign contracts guaranteeing privacy, confidentiality and discretion.

The Wisdom of Solomon is filled with rewards for those who are discrete and confidential. Note this principle found in Proverbs 21:23, "Whoso keepeth his mouth and his tongue keepeth his soul from troubles."

Solomon guarded his focus. He showed no interest in even hearing the criticism from his staff. In Ecclesiastes 7:21, he says, "Also take no heed unto all words that are spoken; lest thou hear thy servant curse thee."

Most of us have struggled with the temptation to dig through the conversations of others in search of one sentence of criticism. Then, use that criticism to build a case against that person and destroy the relationship.

Solomon knew the power and the rewards of focusing on his goal. Nothing was more important to him than the *completion* of his goal—even the criticism from those closest to him.

Solomon rarely discussed his personal life with anyone. The name of his best friend and his favorite people are not even recorded anywhere in history.

Donald Trump wrote on page 24 of his book, "I don't particularly like talking about my personal life...when I do give an interview, I always keep it short. The reporter is in and out in less than twenty minutes."

Successful people limit the access others have to them.

Solomon knew the power of privacy and confidentiality. It is one of the Golden Secrets that helped him to become The Richest Man Who Ever Lived.

～ 30 ～

SOLOMON ONLY HIRED
HAPPY PEOPLE

People Choose To Be Happy.

So, happy people are uncommon decision-makers. They have chosen—deliberately chosen to focus on the good side of life. They are not blind to the thorns. They have chosen to focus on the roses, the good experiences instead.

Most people think that happy people are those experiencing wonderful moments, uncommon financial rewards and deep love from others. Often the opposite is true. Some of the happiest people I know have experienced the deepest sorrows, tragedies and uncommon battles in life. At some point, they made a decision to be a happy person. It is far more than the "personality God gave you at your birth."

Solomon prospered in every direction of his life. One of the most powerful keys was his selection of employees. He knew the importance of selecting those whose countenance he would gaze upon every day.

The Queen of Sheba noted this instantly. As mentioned earlier, her gift to him was $4.5 million. She had traveled by chariot more than 1,000 miles for her moments with King Solomon. She was brilliant, articulate, and a leader of a nation. One of her first observations was to study the people Solomon had selected to wait upon him. She said in 1 Kings 10:8, "Happy are thy men, happy are these thy servants, which stand continually before thee, and that hear thy Wisdom."

▶ Happy people make the decision to *become so.*
▶ Happy people like the decisions they are making.
▶ Happy people are often the best *decision-makers* around you.
▶ Happy people energize *others* to a higher level of productivity and enthusiasm.
▶ Happy people use a completely different *vocabulary* than the unhappy. They say, "We will make it happen!" The unhappy often say, "That's impossible."
▶ Happy people create a climate of *expectation,* not depression.

I read a powerful statement the other day by a famous writer in the business world. He said that the one question necessary to ask a prospective employee is, "If I were to talk to your last boss about you, what would be the first thing he would probably say?" The answer is a photograph of the relationship that person has established with the previous authority figure in his or her life.

What memories in Solomon birthed this remarkable understanding of choosing employees? Many.

He was the son of an illicit relationship. His father, David, had killed the husband of his own mother, Bathsheba. His brother, Absalom, had betrayed and damaged his father irreparably before the nation of Israel. His father's best friend killed his brother. His personal journal was filled with blood baths, conflict and warfare. Attempts to assassinate were common toward his father, King David.

He cherished joy when he entered subsequently into its presence.

So *he only hired happy servants who created the climate he wanted in his palace.* He hated rivalry, conflict and jealousy. So he refused to hire the Miserable, the Fault-Finding and the Fighters.

Solomon only hired happy employees. That's one of the Golden Secrets that helped him become The Richest Man Who Ever Lived.

What You Respect Will Move Toward You.

-MIKE MURDOCK

❧ 31 ❧

SOLOMON WAS HONEST ABOUT THE LIMITATIONS OF HIS WEALTH

Wealth Is Not The Solution To Every Problem In Life.

The poor often imagine that money is the solution to all their problems. The wealthy know better, and yet, thousands of successful people keep lying to themselves about the fantasy of riches. Yet, promotions and raises never satisfy.

Solomon knew this. He was very honest about his times of loneliness. He had 700 wives and 300 concubines surrounding him. Children pulled at his heart daily. In fact everyone clamored for his attention. And yet, we find no name in any of the ancient writings about Solomon of even one close personal friend in his life.

He was honest about his seasons of depression. In Ecclesiastes 2:17, he wrote, "Therefore I hated life."

Solomon knew that money could not purchase eternal life on earth. Note his words from Ecclesiastes 12:7, "Then shall the dust return to the earth as it was: and the spirit shall return unto God who gave it."

He knew how fleeting riches could be. He says in Proverbs 23:5, "Wilt thou set thine eyes upon that which is not? for riches certainly make themselves wings; they fly away as an eagle toward Heaven." He also wrote in Proverbs 27:24, "For riches are not for ever."

He knew that the appetite for accumulation could rule and ruin a man. In Proverbs 27:20, he says, "Hell and destruction are never full; so the eyes of man are never satisfied."

This is a powerful secret of Solomon's life. He did not lie to himself, nor did he lie to others. He was truthful and honest. It made him more vulnerable, fragile and might have threatened the mystique and charisma of his presence. But this was *one of the secrets of his greatness.*

Solomon did not hide his weaknesses, his emotions or his feelings of futility. He faced them, described them, and wrote about them. Speaking from seasons of loneliness and insecurity, he was able to unlock answers and solutions. It was this kind of integrity that brought him to the appropriate and accurate conclusion of life which is recorded in Ecclesiastes 12:13-14, "Let us hear the conclusion of the whole matter: Fear God, and keep his commandments: for this is the whole duty of man. For God shall bring every work into judgment, with every secret thing, whether it be good, or whether it be evil."

▶ When you admit your hunger, *food will come to you.*

▶ When you admit you are thirsty, *water will flow quickly in your direction.*

▶ When you confess your confusion, answers will swiftly emerge.

▶ *What you respect will move toward you.*

▶ *What you do not respect will move away from you.* It may be friends, Wisdom or money.

One of the most important success secrets you will ever unlock during your lifetime is the ability to recognize the incredible, irreplaceable and gratifying gifts that money *cannot* purchase on earth.

Wealth can purchase a house.

Wisdom makes it a *harbor*.

Wealth purchases favors.

Wisdom creates *favor*.

Wealth determines possessions.

Wisdom determines *peace*.

Wealth can hire companionship.

Wisdom births *commitment*.

Wealth can hire a listener.

Wisdom generates *love*.

Wealth may hide a weakness.

Wisdom *removes it*.

Wealth has its limitations. Solomon recognized this Golden Secret and, he became The Richest Man Who Ever Lived.

DECISION

Will You Accept Jesus As Your Personal Savior Today?

The Bible says, "That if thou shalt confess with thy mouth the Lord Jesus, and shalt believe in thine heart that God hath raised Him from the dead, thou shalt be saved," (Romans 10:9).

Pray this prayer from your heart today!

"Dear Jesus, I believe that You died for me and rose again on the third day. I confess I am a sinner...I need Your love and forgiveness...Come into my heart. Forgive my sins. I receive Your eternal life. Confirm Your love by giving me peace, joy and supernatural love for others. Amen."

DR. MIKE MURDOCK

is in tremendous demand as one of the most dynamic speakers in America today.

More than 17,000 audiences in over 100 countries have attended his Schools of Wisdom and conferences. Hundreds of invitations come to him from churches, colleges and business corporations. He is a noted author of over 250 books, including the best sellers, *The Leadership Secrets of Jesus* and *Secrets of the Richest Man Who Ever Lived.* Thousands view his weekly television program, *Wisdom Keys with Mike Murdock.* Many attend his Schools of Wisdom that he hosts in many cities of America.

CLIP AND MAIL

DR. MIKE MURDOCK

1 Has embraced his Assignment to Pursue...Proclaim...and Publish the Wisdom of God to help people achieve their dreams and goals.

2 Preached his first public sermon at the age of 8.

3 Preached his first evangelistic crusade at the age of 15.

4 Began full-time evangelism at the age of 19, which has continued since 1966.

5 Has traveled and spoken to more than 17,000 audiences in over 100 countries, including East and West Africa, Asia, Europe and South America.

6 Noted author of over 250 books, including best sellers, *Wisdom for Winning, Dream Seeds, The Double Diamond Principle, The Law of Recognition* and *The Holy Spirit Handbook.*

7 Created the popular *Topical Bible* series for Businessmen, Mothers, Fathers, Teenagers; *The One-Minute Pocket Bible* series, and *The Uncommon Life* series.

8 The Creator of The Master 7 Mentorship System, an Achievement Program for Believers.

9 Has composed thousands of songs such as "I Am Blessed," "You Can Make It," "God Rides On Wings of Love" and "Jesus, Just The Mention of Your Name," recorded by many gospel artists.

10 Is the Founder and Senior Pastor of The Wisdom Center, in Fort Worth, Texas...a Church with International Ministry around the world.

11 Host of *Wisdom Keys with Mike Murdock,* a weekly TV Program seen internationally.

12 Has appeared often on TBN, CBN, BET, Daystar, Inspirational Network, LeSea Broadcasting and other television network programs.

13 Has led over 3,000 to accept the call into full-time ministry.

THE MINISTRY

1 **Wisdom Books & Literature** - Over 250 best-selling Wisdom Books and 70 Teaching Tape Series.

2 **Church Crusades** - Multitudes are ministered to in crusades and seminars throughout America in "The Uncommon Wisdom Conferences." Known as a man who loves pastors, he has focused on church crusades for over 43 years.

3 **Music Ministry** - Millions have been blessed by the anointed songwriting and singing of Mike Murdock, who has made over 15 music albums and CDs available.

4 **Television** - *Wisdom Keys with Mike Murdock,* a nationally-syndicated weekly television program.

5 **The Wisdom Center** - The Church and Ministry Offices where Dr. Murdock speaks weekly on Wisdom for The Uncommon Life.

6 **Schools of The Holy Spirit** - Mike Murdock hosts Schools of The Holy Spirit in many churches to mentor believers on the Person and Companionship of The Holy Spirit.

7 **Schools of Wisdom** - In many major cities Mike Murdock hosts Schools of Wisdom for those who want personalized and advanced training for achieving "The Uncommon Dream."

8 **Missions Outreach** - Dr. Mike Murdock's overseas outreaches to over 100 countries have included crusades in East and West Africa, Asia, Europe and South America.

CPSIA information can be obtained
at www.ICGtesting.com
Printed in the USA
LVOW10s2326310517
536527LV00036B/1172/P